THE **SPIRITUAL**
ALCHEMIST

Working with the Voice of Your Soul

THE SPIRITUAL
ALCHEMIST

Working with the Voice of Your Soul

NATALIE REID

RIVER DAUGHTER PRESS

The Spiritual Alchemist: Working with the Voice of Your Soul

published by
River Daughter Press
P.O. Box 20396
Albuquerque, New Mexico 87154-0396
www.thespiritualalchemist.com

First printing 2008

cover art: Charl Agiza
cover and book design: Judith Schwartz, Witz End Design

Reid, Natalie
The spiritual alchemist : working with the voice of your soul / Natalie Reid

ISBN 978-0-615-18196-7 (pb.)

Printed in the United States of America

10 9 8 7 6 5 4 3 2 1

To Ruth Abrass,
friend, colleague, and
spiritual energy healer extraordinaire

Table of Contents

Acknowledgments

The path of spiritual alchemy, while ultimately personal and individual, is never solitary. We are led to it by teachers, friends, and fellow alchemists, many of whom accompany us along the way. To all my friends and teachers in this lifetime—some still living, some not—I offer my heartfelt gratitude.

Those involved in the birth of this book are likewise many, and I am grateful to them all. Mary Roach planted the seed for the workshop out of which the book evolved. Many writing groups, ritual groups, women's groups, religious institutions, retreat centers, artists colonies, private groups, centers for the arts, and schools of transpersonal psychology and holistic studies have sponsored the workshop—and among those whom I thank for leading me to them are Judith Behrendt, Marsha Browne, Robin Chapman, Marilyn Zembo Day, Jill Egland, Michelle Gallant, Linda Hart, Dixie King, Cynthia Laitman, Anne Schneider, and Erica Weick.

Thanks beyond measure go to that phenomenal visionary, Hannelore Hahn, founder and director of the International Women's Writing Guild. Her faith in my work introduced me to the annual IWWG writing conference on the Skidmore College campus— a world of women writers, agents, workshop directors, and artists unmatched in my experience for creativity, commitment, mutual support, artistic integrity, and sheer talent. Among the many workshop directors, I thank Pat Carr, Diane Gallo, Carol Peck, and Eunice Scarfe for helping me hone my skills as a writer, as well as Alice Orr and Liz Aleshire for teaching me the business of writing.

The Spiritual Alchemist went through several drafts, the first of which I wrote at the Writers Colony at Dairy Hollow in Eureka Springs, AR—a peaceful writing sanctuary in a community of writers. Great thanks to Mildred Lynn McDonald and Bill Murphy for their helpful suggestions and discerning comments on that draft—and especially to Mildred Lynn for a particular piece of advice that later helped me complete the book. I wrote the second draft in Tahlequah, OK, where I lived in the woods in the Cedar House and had the good fortune of getting to know proprietors Al and Frankie Herrin.

With immense gratitude I thank my five readers—Ruth Abrass, Charl Agiza, Yael Flusberg, Gail Harris, and Paula Mate—for generosity of time and spirit, and for focused and detailed editorial comments. All writers should be fortunate enough to have such friends.

I am also grateful to publishing coach Melissa Rosati for her savvy advice and encouragement; to Judith Schwartz of Witz End Design for her design skills and experience; and again to friend and artist Charl Agiza for the use of her painting, *The Journey*, for the cover.

Spiraling back to the beginning, I thank and honor my parents, Harold Reid (may his memory be for a blessing) and Gloria Reid. Thank you, Harold, for showing me—by how you lived your life—what it truly means to be a teacher. Thank you, Gloria, for encouraging me to write from early childhood and for buying me that gorgeous leather-bound journal all those years ago, when you couldn't really afford the expense. Thanks to Howard Schwartz, Rabbi Gershon Winkler, and other writer friends and teachers for your faith in my gifts, and to Dr. Kenneth J. Emonds for being who you are and for saving my life. And thanks beyond words to nearly lifelong friend and sister Ruth Abrass, without whose wisdom, integrity, love, and spiritual gifts I would not stand in the place I stand now.

Finally, my wholehearted gratitude and respect go to the many magnificent spiritual alchemists who have participated in the workshop and whose honest, insightful experiences round out the teaching and bring the process to life. *The Spiritual Alchemist* is as much theirs as mine.

All seekers are spiritual alchemists in the making.

If you wish to hear the voice of your own soul and to learn from it why you are here and what work you have come to do, this book is for you. It will guide you through ten steps that are easy to do yet profound in the ways in which they will alter your perception of yourself and the world around you.

As you engage with and enjoy the process (or, perhaps, be challenged by it), you will change. You will become not only an alchemist in your own life but also *the* alchemist of your own life. The path of spiritual alchemy, once taken, becomes yours forever.

May this book help you to walk that path in grace and joy.

PART ONE

THE PROCESS

because it is infused with the divine, and that every action on earth either diminishes or adds to the divine source from which we come and to which we will eventually return. The alchemists who attempted to transmute base metals into gold viewed their tiny laboratories as microcosms of a greater laboratory, one in which they—along with all of creation—were the subjects of a larger experiment: that of transforming baser human desires into more refined ones that brought them, through their soul, closer to the divine.

Alchemists didn't want to merely transform lead into gold. They wanted to crack the code, to read the divine writing hidden in all material substances, to uncover the divine intent in every organic and inorganic thing. They sought to align physical energies with the source of all universal divine energies. The more their chemical processes matured, the more profoundly they felt the confluence of the chemical and the spiritual, the convergence of the material and the ethereal. The harder they worked "below," the deeper their connection—and the closer they believed that they came—to the divine "above."

While many think of alchemy as a lost practice of the past, it has simply lain dormant in some places, gone underground in others, turned into chemistry in the sciences, and remained a spiritual practice in a number of the world's mystical traditions. The great twentieth century psychologist Carl Jung studied and wrote about alchemy, incorporating its symbols and processes into his thinking and his work. Elements of alchemy are therefore present in the physical sciences, in psychology, and in religious and spiritual practice. The spirit of alchemy continues to draw—however unconsciously—all those who seek to regain their connection with the voice of their own divine soul.

WHAT IS A SPIRITUAL ALCHEMIST?

I believe that we can all learn to become spiritual alchemists in our own lives—to learn why we are here and how best to honor our soul's unique purpose in the way we live. To learn to set our life's compass, as the ancients did, by our soul's intent. To create form out of the chaos of our emotional lives, so that we can harmonize impulse and act.

A spiritual alchemist is a person who seeks to be the best person he or she can be, not for the sake of fame or fortune but for the sake of living rightly. A person who models his or her life on the principle of "as above, so below," wishing that "thy will," not "my [petty or controlling or self-serving] will" be done. A person who wishes to serve that which is good in his or her unique fashion—and to nurture and honor that uniqueness along the way. In essence, spiritual alchemists are people who yearn to deepen their connection to the "above"—to the divine—and who are willing to take the risk of being their own persons, no matter what the cost "below," in their desire to maintain that connection.

A spiritual alchemist is who you want to be, if your goal is to reunite your daily, mundane consciousness with that of your soul, so that everything you do is informed and guided by your soul's intent.

Whenever a person holds a belief deeply, he or she will do whatever is necessary to act in harmony with it. Ancient and medieval alchemists were sustained by belief, which gave them the patience they needed for alchemy's complex processes. The very word "alchemy" has come to imply process, and any process, of course, always demands patience. To become a spiritual alchemist means to develop a new process, one that allows us to reach the purest individual source of divine wisdom, inspiration, and creativity that each of us has. We need to allow it to change us from people who hear with only our ears into people who can also hear the silent "still small voice" of our soul. To learn this process, then we, too—like all alchemists—need to start with patience.

But patience is a scarce commodity in the West, where we are always looking for a quick fix. We say we're not, of course. We say that we're on a spiritual journey and tell ourselves that we believe in growth and process. But every time we pick up a new book or take a new workshop, we secretly hope that this one will do the trick. This time we will find the real answers. This time we will experience the "aha" moment that makes everything clear, that frees us of our fears and permanently dissipates our doubts. This one, we think, will contain the magic elixir that changes us forever.

Yet a genuine "aha" moment is a sudden recognition of something important that we have needed to know, a realization or revelation from which we can then continue to grow. A spiritual fix, on the other hand, is the illusion of having so permanently received *the* answer that the growing is finally done or that true enlightenment has arrived. True process, however, accepts and values the "aha" moments without calcifying them; it allows them to sink in along the way, as part of a continuing, wondrous, and never-ending journey.

We believe in process, we tell ourselves—but all the while, we are secretly looking for that spiritual fix.

What alchemy teaches is commitment to process: to commit ourselves to the process of change, from the imperfect towards perfection, all the while knowing that the process will take a lifetime and will never fully end. We are here, after all, not to learn to be saints but to learn to be human.

Carl Jung, the best known of the twentieth century alchemists, was most likely a gnostic ("knower," from the Greek *gnosis*), following the ancient tradition of knowing truth by accepting and holding the tensions between the opposites in nature, including human nature. Gnostics did not believe in trying to rid the self of the negative, because they believed it both impossible and unwise. Jung, like the gnostics before him, viewed alchemy as a spiritual discipline devoted to the mediation and unification of both material and spiritual opposites. These opposites included both the physical polarities (soft and hard, cold and hot) and the emotional ones (love and fear, attraction and repulsion).

According to Jung, the mediator between the material and the spiritual—and between the ever-present tension of spiritual opposites—would always be the imagination. In other words, our ability to imagine ourselves in different ways, and to envision our positive and negative qualities interacting differently with one another in our daily lives, holds the key to genuine self-knowledge. Ultimately, it is in the imagination that we all must start our journey into spiritual alchemy—not an imagination of make-believe but an imagination that allows us to create anew, to see through different lenses, to revision our world.

I wrote this book to take you through that imaginal journey into spiritual alchemy. The deceptively simple process requires only your being willing to imagine and being willing to develop or further develop patience. From the springboard of these two desires, you can launch yourself into a journey that will take you to your private inner laboratory, the divine space that has been waiting for you since you were born. Like the "chemical" alchemist, the spiritual alchemist also has a laboratory—one that lies not in physical space but inside you, at the core of who you are.

"But why is the space *inside* us?" some people ask. "Why isn't it out in nature or in a house of worship?"

The answer is that we all have to begin with ourselves. The basic principle of alchemy—"as above, so below"—teaches us to deal with ourselves as divinely inspirited beings living in material bodies. We are in bodies—"embodied"—for a reason. For all that we may feel "one" with nature, be "one" with the universe, or see our bodies as illusions, we still live in bodies. We still have the physical boundaries (skin and bones) that separate us from others. No differently from physical or chemical alchemy, spiritual alchemy demands that we hold and respect the ongoing tension between the spiritual and the material—not ignore it. When we choose to develop spiritually in bodies, as human beings with individual strengths and weaknesses, we must do so *through ourselves as we are.*

The inner laboratory you will be creating, therefore, mirrors the human condition—your limits, your boundaries, your separateness. Just as your body houses your spirit, your inner laboratory will contain your strengths, weaknesses, and potential—the best and worst of you as you experience yourself at this moment.

Only by accepting our physical separateness, and acknowledging our longing not to be separate, can we honor our personal uniqueness. Only by knowing ourselves more intimately—and honestly—can we begin to communicate clearly with our larger soul.

Just as ancient alchemists used physical vessels for their work, spiritual alchemists recognize, through self-honesty and self-love, that we are sacred vessels. Ultimately, we touch our own sanctity best when we go within ourselves, into our inner laboratory, for the purpose of connecting with the divine of which we are a part.

We will do so through a process I will teach you, a process grounded in love, hope, and sustenance. If we want to listen to the voice of our own soul, we need to realize that listening and love—self-love—are intricately connected. The more we begin to love ourselves (not with mere words but deeply and truly), the more we can listen—and listen well, without interference—to that voice. Loving ourselves, of course, involves recognizing and accepting all the pairs of opposites, the so-called "bad" with the good. Learning to listen to the voice of our own soul comes through love; believing that we can do it comes through hope; and making it work comes through what I call *sustenance*—that is, sustaining both the love and the hope. The process of sustenance is one of commitment—and it is through sustaining commitment that we alchemists come closer and closer to our goal.

WHAT IS A SOUL?

Alchemy texts dating back thousands of years, whether giving instructions for finding the secret of immortality or transmuting lead into gold, also indicate the parallel goal of attempting to perfect the soul by attempting to perfect the self. But what exactly did alchemists mean by "soul"? Because different alchemical traditions arose from different religious and ethnic cultures, and therefore have different ways of framing the concept of soul, I choose to speak from the ancient heritage to which I belong and from which my understanding of soul consciousness derives: the Jewish tradition. Throughout this book my references to Jewish beliefs, Hebrew words, or the mystical interpretation of biblical tales are intended to deepen and broaden our understanding of soul consciousness and the practice of spiritual alchemy.

In the Jewish tradition, the divine is unknowable: Our human minds are too limited to comprehend the vastness and wonder of the divine mind or the divine plan. God, as such, is beyond us. However, as we are created by the divine and therefore part of it, we can come to "touch" the divine—but indirectly, through our connection with our individual soul.

Unlike English, Hebrew has no single word for soul. Instead, it has five distinct words (*nefesh, ruach, neshama, chaya, yechida*), each signifying a different level of spiritual evolution. At the highest level (*yechida*), our spiritual consciousness is one with the divine, inseparable from God-consciousness. According to the mystical tradition, this level of soul has sent a part of itself—you—to this lifetime of learning, to continue perfecting

My workshop experience has shown me that using this approach, with no mental preparation, works best. The more you allow the process to unfold naturally, from the unconscious, imaginative parts of your being, the more it will lead you to new discoveries. The more you trust the process, the more authentic an inner laboratory you will create. I've actually nicknamed this workshop my "stealth workshop," because the exercises sneak up on people with a cumulative effect that usually surprises, invigorates, and delights them.

If, however, your style has always been to try to get the lay of the land, to make sure that you do things "right," keep in mind that these exercises have no right and wrong answers. There is no teacher or parent to please. For spiritual alchemy, trying to "do it right" actually causes unnecessary stress—the fear of "doing it wrong." Because that fear exacerbates people's unconscious needs for control, those who manage to break free of that pattern often get the greatest benefit. So if you know that you still need to please authority, or that you're a highly analytical person who needs to know "why" before doing anything, this process offers you the chance to release those needs. By calling for courage, spiritual alchemy also calls for you to take a leap into a new way of doing and being.

Be sure to start all of the exercises in the following way:
- Sit upright and close your eyes.
- Then concentrate on breathing out, for at least three to five deep, long breaths.

Obviously, to breathe out, you have to first have breathed in. The point of concentrating on breathing out is that it focuses you on emptying yourself. By concentrating on breathing out, you begin forming your intention to make space for new ways of seeing and new ways of being.

As you will be writing either during these exercises or immediately afterwards, always have pen and paper or a journal handy before you begin. Each exercise has a clock icon with an indication of how long it might take, so you can plan your time accordingly. The CD that comes with the book contains ten very short guided visualizations for Exercises 5-8, so for those exercises you also need a CD player. (The instructions for the visualizations also appear at the end of the book.)

You can take an entire day to do all the exercises, do one or two an evening, do one a day for ten days, or use any other variation that suits you. Still, the shorter the time between the first and the last exercise, the more intense your experience is likely to be.

When you begin doing the exercises, you can do them alone, in the privacy of your own home, or with a close friend or a group of trusted friends. I highly recommend learning to use these tools for spiritual alchemy with at least one other person whom you fully trust. Throughout the book you'll discover even more fully the importance of doing the work with trusted others.

I repeat "trust" and "trusted" for a reason: Your first important decision in this life-changing work is to know who wants to do this kind of work and with whom it is *safe* for you to do it. For example, many people who begin transformational work want their spouses or significant others to share the experiences with them. Too often, these partners are people whom the person wants to change (a very bad idea, as nobody can ever change anybody). Too often, these partners are not interested in transforming themselves—and their unwilling or resistant presence will ruin the experience for the person who wants to do it. As self-honesty is one of the keys to becoming a spiritual alchemist, you must be honest with yourself about whom you are safest with when learning to listen to the voice of your own soul.

Doing this work with people you trust will bring you not only safety and joy but also a wealth of new insights. With a "soul-searching" partner or group of friends, you will help one another along your individual paths. As commonly happens, if each of you does an exercise differently, then you each help the others expand your collective understanding of what the exercise offers. Working together heightens the experience and amplifies your self-discoveries.

On the other hand, doing the work alone brings riches that you can later share with others. Each of you walks your own path; each of you knows how best to proceed.

The only other chapter you may need to know about now is the one that will help you if you find yourself encountering huge resistance, as in "*I don't want to do this!!*" If that happens, turn to Chapter 10, to read about the nature of resistance and the powerful insights that result from staying the course. Otherwise, do the exercises first and read the chapters in sequence.

As you read, and as you do the exercises, know that you are never alone. I'm not only speaking about the presence of your soul. I'm also speaking about the many workshop participants who have sent me copies of their notes and journal entries, descriptions of their discoveries, and messages from their souls. They will also be walking with you. Their stories, their questions, their interactions, and their insights will soon become yours.

PART TWO

THE EXERCISES

Sharing names, "forgetting" names

When the fifteen minutes are up, everybody wants to talk:

"I can't believe what this list is telling me."

("Hold that thought. We'll get to it later.")

"Most of the names I don't like came from other people."

("Hold that thought....")

"I'd forgotten I used to think of myself as a saint."

"You were a saint? So was I!"

Lots of things happen when we start talking about our names. Often we discover common names. In one workshop, for example, three of us were the family scapegoat; a third of us thought to name ourselves according to our ethnic origins; and half the parents were called "control freaks" by their children but wouldn't use the term for themselves. While shared names are sometimes the beginning of a harmonizing or synchronizing of participant energy, just as often they are common archetypes or themes that run through the naming process. (If, say, 20 of the women have children and most of them put "nurturer" on their lists, that's no surprise.)

As people talk about their lists, some realize that they forgot to include an important name. "Forgetting" is an extremely useful gift. It alerts us that something within us has shifted or is shifting. For example, before giving my first workshop, I tested this exercise with my close friend Ruth, who at the time was working with abused women both in and out of a local shelter. When she read her list aloud, I was impressed.

"You put down all sorts of things I didn't even think about," I said, "like 'daughter' and 'wife' and 'sister'—all those relationship words. And the words about spiritual awakening.... Next to yours, my list feels really incomplete."

But as I read mine to her and reached the word "feminist," she let out a yell and did something I thought happened only in fiction: She nearly leaped out of her chair.

"How could I have forgotten 'feminist'?! I've been calling myself a feminist for over seven years, I work with women, I see the world through a feminist lens."

As we went back over her list, which included "Buddhist" and "spiritual being," I voiced a sudden thought: "You're moving into a new phase of your development. Maybe you didn't have to write down 'feminist' because it's become such a part of you that it informs everything you do. You've become a feminist so deeply and completely that it no longer comes up as a name."

She thought about it, then nodded. "You're right. I don't need to focus on the word anymore, to help me be conscious of what I want to become. Feminist is what I am."

"Forgetting" may signal a part of ourselves that has become so well integrated in our lives that it doesn't appear on our list. As you read some of the names in this chapter, you may realize that you, too, forgot an important name. If so, pay attention. Something is about to shift in your life—and probably for the good.

Emergent Names

Kate raises her hand. "I got a bunch of new names with a similar theme running through them. What does that mean?"

Kate gives us her new names: "landmark, guide, lantern, lamppost." In the margin she has written, "I shine the light onto the path, like a tour guide. I provide landmarks— emotional, spiritual, intellectual, and physical."

We ask about her present situation. She tells us she is about to open a healing center, where healers and energy workers can gather to help people in her community. Everyone starts laughing that wonderful good-natured laughter that bubbles up when people recognize the obvious. Her center will be the "landmark" where people come for healing.

Names that come out of the blue fascinate people. New names—anything from "Artemisia" to "driftwood," from "clown" to "tumbled turquoise"—herald transformation. The first time I ran across such names was while Ruth and I were testing this exercise. Her list included several odd names that "just came in." Not only did we wonder what they meant, but I felt disappointed at not receiving any.

I now understand them as *emergent* names, names emerging out of our unconscious selves and about to show up in what we call our personality. Emergent names signal an unconscious aspect of yourself that wants to become a conscious part of your life. When such names appear on your list, they are signposts, forerunners of new directions or new behavior patterns.

For example, perhaps a woman thinks of herself as a slowpoke. But if "greased lightning" or "mercury" or "in the fast lane"—or all three!—turns up on her list, she can expect to soon be hearing from the speedy part of herself that her slowpoke self-image never allowed her to experience.

In another instance, when Darlene writes down the name "enveloper," she doesn't understand it. At a later stage in the process, she asks her soul to tell her what it means. The profound answer astonishes her:

> Enveloper: One whose spirit envelops and infuses the spirits of others,
> that their consciousness be elevated and stimulated, that their self-
> awareness be heightened, that their self-connection be strengthened, and
> that their consciousness of their connection with the divine be deepened.
> The enveloper spreads her "wings" over the group. The enveloper casts the

net of her aura over the group—and knows when and how to carefully, silently, withdraw it, leaving the newly planted seeds behind.

After working with the naming process for so many years, I too get the occasional emergent name. Some are poetic and somewhat vague, like *ally of truth*. Others relate more obviously to my current emotional state, such as *one who doesn't suffer fools lightly* when I'm trying to correct a billing error with a person who keeps repeating "but it's in the computer...."

Emergent names aren't necessarily permanent. They may represent a self that shows up for a brief time, then vanishes—or a name that comes and goes, reemerging in your life when needed. Others may appear only once but are usually right on target. One person said that the strangest one-time name she ever heard was *inferno of chaos*. When she later asked her soul voice for an explanation, she heard:

> This is the churning of the yearning, the grieving, and the rage that comes with violent endings and beginnings. The phoenix rises out of ashes, but you have no patience to wait for the fire to die. Therefore, you are an inferno right now, letting chaos reside in you until you have burned it up, so that only your personal flame, the flame of your own passion, burns clearly in you again.

Both the name and the answer puzzled her greatly. True, she was grieving a miscarriage and furious with her husband over his lack of sympathy with her tears. But the whole message felt strange to her—and the "inferno" sounded too huge, too powerful, too all-encompassing for what she called "reasonable grief and anger."

Three weeks later she was diagnosed with two kinds of cancer.

Learning from Emergent Names

The meaning of an emergent name rarely makes itself completely known during a workshop—or while we are doing the exercise itself. We usually have to take the names home and sit with them until they reveal themselves fully. This means spending quiet time with the new name. People who have done this work report valuable insights. Pauline writes:

> I began with the "normal" names, and then some not-so-normal names began to pop up. One of these was "Hobo Fly".... At the time I felt it was probably just something weird.
>
> I know now the meaning of "Hobo Fly." It has to do with my life. A hobo goes from one place to another, either from necessity or choice, and experiences many things. She usually travels alone but meets many interesting

events and people—never knowing what she might encounter but somehow trusting that it will be as it should be.

This has been a long-fought lesson for me. For such a long time I felt that others must believe as I do…for what was happening to me to be valid. However, I now understand that no matter how many people are in my life or agree with me, much of my life journey will be alone, and it needs no validation to be my true experience. Probably because I am allowing more, I am experiencing so many things that up until now I could not even imagine. Now I am indeed flying. It is wonderful being a Hobo Fly.

A year or two later, Pauline sends me a letter asking to be kept informed about my workshop schedule. She will soon be able to come to any number of cities, she writes, because she is taking flying lessons.

WORKING WITH MYTH

Carl Jung used the phrase "collective unconscious" to describe the origin of symbols common to humanity. Because we all drink from this communal well, we often understand one another's dreams and dream symbols.

But individual cultures also include symbols quite specific to them. In the English-speaking West, for example, Scrooge symbolizes hard-hearted greed and miserliness, while "he's an angel" tells us that a man goes out of his way to do good for others. For those of us who have read classical literature—who know the classic Greek or Roman, Nordic or Hindu god-stories like the backs of our hands—these figures carry valuable information.

Penelope Bourk's emergent name was "Demophoon." In Greek mythology, Demophoon is an infant prince at Eleusis. His mother finds him a nurse, who turns out to be the earth goddess Demeter in disguise. (Eleusis is also the place of the Eleusinian mysteries, a sacred rite of initiation and spiritual rebirth for women in ancient Greece.)

I invite you into the complexity of Penelope's discoveries, to see the powerful insights that emergent names can bring us when we sit with them long enough. She writes:

> What Demophoon's mother did not yet know is that a goddess nurses differently than a mortal mother. Each night, Demeter would lower the infant into the hearth fire to burn off his mortality. One night the mother happened to witness this event, and, horrified at the sight of the child in the fire, attacked the goddess, who flung the child out of the fire, and hence away from immortality.
>
> "So what has Demophoon to do with me?" I wondered after this writing exercise in your class.

making vertical lists. Their creative work has taught me three other ways of arranging, all of which I happily pass on to you: circles, spirals, and trees.

To arrange by circles, you might start by arranging the longest duration names in the center circle, then putting the other names in larger concentric circles until you have an outer circle with all the shortest-duration or emergent names. Or you might do the opposite, if that appeals to you: putting all the shortest-duration names in the center, and ending up with the big outermost circle holding the names that have lasted the longest and still "encircle" you.

To arrange by spirals, put the longest-duration names at the center of the spiral and then work outwards, so that the newest names are at the widest end of the spiral.

As for the tree-makers, they create *trees of the self*. To arrange by "tree," draw a large tree with a wide trunk. Then arrange your names like this:
- The lifelong names go in the roots.
- The names of many years go in the trunk.
- The names of fewer years form the main branches.
- The even shorter-lasting names form the small branches.
- The emergent names become the leaves.

As you arrange, enjoy your choice of vertical lists, circles, spirals, or trees. But if you find yourself heading towards another arrangement, go with it. For example, David, a French horn player and music teacher, found himself arranging his names into a musical score. He later wrote that he always views his life in terms of music and composition, and that arranging the names musically gave him a sense of his entire life:

> My life...suddenly looked like the rich score of a full symphonic piece...
> and I hear it all as music. Some events and people have been discordant,
> some richly harmonic. Sometimes the orchestration and the direction have
> been so dense and confusing, if you were listening you would hardly know
> where the piece was going...but it was going somewhere intentional....The
> Big Composer, I suppose...?

After you have used *duration* throughout the entire three-part technique, I'll show you how to apply the technique to every part of your life. From then on, you can choose whether to arrange by list, circle, spirals, trees, or any other creation of your own beautiful imagination. I'll also give you instructions for the other two types of arranging. The following chapter will show you how to apply both.

You may have noticed that this chapter contains almost no stories or examples. That's because arranging is the "hinge" step, between the first and third steps.

So get ready for step three: *Patterning.*

Knowing Yourself:
Patterning

The third part of the three-part technique is called *Patterning*. As the heart of alchemy is the search for patterns, this work involves finding patterns in your arranged list.

You may have already started patterning without realizing it, because you may have noticed some patterns while doing the arranging. For example, maybe you found that names from your childhood evoke different feelings than your more recent names. Or maybe you noticed that other people's names for you feel positive, while your names for yourself feel negative—or the opposite.

While some people are very good at finding patterns, others have a little more difficulty. If patterning doesn't come easily to you, relax. It's a skill that you can learn, no differently from the way you learned to tie your shoelaces, do jigsaw puzzles, or work with new computer software.

Think of it this way: Since all of these names are or were yours, they are all related to you in some way. Therefore, some of them—and maybe all of them—are also related to each other in some way. You are the only person who can figure out the connections.

Keep in mind that no two people find the same pattern—and that there is no particular or perfect pattern you are "supposed" to find. Just remember that every arranged list has at least one pattern in it—and probably more.

EXERCISE 1C

Patterning Your Names

EXERCISE 1C

Patterning

 5 to 15 minutes

1. Look for patterns in your *arranged* list.

> *Helpful Hint*
>
> The patterns may be emotional, mental, or visual.
>
> - With emotional patterns, you find that certain groups or types of names make you feel positive or negative, happy or sad.
>
> - With mental patterns, you may find that the names in one part of the list—top, bottom, middle—are connected by the same theme or idea.
>
> - With visual patterns, you find that the actual words (as they appear on the page) form the shape of an object.

2. Write down the patterns that you've noticed and how they make you feel.

3. Write down any new insights, whether about yourself or your relationship to others, that emerged from doing the patterning.

> *Helpful Hint*
>
> If you have never done patterning before and still feel stuck after trying, read the rest of this chapter first, to find some tips. Or, if you're doing this exercise with a group, ask the others for help. Once you get the idea, you'll start finding patterns everywhere—in your friendships, in your likes and dislikes, in everything.

4. When you've finished your patterning, continue reading.

PATTERNING

Before the participants finish arranging—before I can even introduce the idea of patterning—many are already finding patterns in their lists. Arranging leads so naturally to pattern-finding that "ooh's" and "aha's," comments about patterns, and probing questions fill the room:

"I can't believe what I'm seeing here."

"Omigod, those awful names aren't mine! They all came from my parents."

"Why are my 'oldest' names the most depressing?"

Patterning, in this case, simply means looking for patterns in your arranged list—seeing what jumps out at you and discovering what patterns reveal themselves in the new arrangement.

By arranging your names according to categories that you would ordinarily not consider, you begin to see yourself in a new light—the light of the patterns facing you on the page. By *patterning* your rearranged list, you allow new understandings of yourself to emerge. You also interrupt and break down your old patterns of viewing yourself. Most important, by disrupting that old self-image, you make room for something new. You make room for alchemy.

Patterning from the three different types of arranging always leads to interesting—and often very different—insights.

PATTERNING A "DURATION" LIST

Here are the kinds of patterning insights that result when people arrange their names according to duration:

> The "five-year duration" section was full of definitions about what I do. It turns out that what I did or do occurs in five-year segments.

> I saw that most of the negative names had been given me by people who didn't know me very well, and the experience with those people and the names they gave me were of short duration.

> Some of the shortest moments were the most up (fun) or down (depressing).

> I don't believe this! There was this man who always loomed large in my life. He took up a huge chunk of my energy, and I always thought he took up a huge chunk of my life. But when I sat down and added it up, I was only with him for one year and one night!

As these few examples show, no one-size-fits-all pattern exists. People discover what they need to discover—just as you may have already.

OTHER ARRANGING METHODS

Now that you have practiced naming, arranging, and patterning according to *duration*, I am going to introduce you to the two other methods of arranging: *chronology* and *hope*.

ARRANGING BY CHRONOLOGY

Chronology is an obvious form of arranging: All you have to do is ask yourself one question—which names applied to me at which times in my life?—and you have a chronological arrangement.

But arranging, say, 40 or 50 names in one chronological list is impractical. If you have a long list, it helps if you make several lists side by side:

- Make one list for names lasting many years (*daughter, younger brother, lifelong nickname*).
- Make another list for names of fewer—but substantial—years (*student, competitive athlete, foster parent*).
- Make yet another list for short-lived names (*nickname lasting only a few months, hobby you took up for only three weeks, emergent names*).

Because many of these names will overlap one another during your lifetime, they will also overlap on a timeline. You will find it easier to see the overlaps if you make several lists. For example, you may have been a high school student at the same time you were *teacher's pet*, *table tennis champion*, and *Goo-goo Eyes*.

> **Helpful Hint**
>
> If you're not sure of certain years (did I date so-and-so, who called me "Honeybuns," in the mid-90s or late 90s?), let your intuition guide you. Instead of obsessing over details, have fun!

Steps for arranging by chronology:

1. Take a good-sized piece of paper, and prepare to make a timeline of your life.

2. Put birth at the bottom left and your present age at the top left. Then prepare to make several vertical lists to the right of it.

3. Make one list (for the appropriate years) of lifelong names.

4. To the right of that, accurately list the names that covered big chunks of your life.

5. To the right of that, list the names that covered fewer years.

For example, let's say you've identified yourself as a member of a certain religion and a daughter or son for your entire life. Those two names would go on your left-hand list. To the right of that list, you might put *spouse* or *partner* if you've been together with someone for a long time, or *friend* or *lover* or *writer* or [*name of profession*] if those names apply to you over a lot of years. Then, to the right of that, you might list *chess player* or *dancer* (if those were roles you played for only a few years) or the name of a job you had or a family role you played for a relatively short time.

PATTERNING A CHRONOLOGICAL LIST

Although patterning by chronology is the least common form of arranging, here are some examples of people's "chronological" discoveries:

> I have always been a writer and a misfit.

> I stopped defining myself in terms of men and my relationship to them when I started working.

> Words and names that other people called me dropped out of my list (that is, out of my consciousness) around the time I started meditating.

> I stopped being a "nonconformist" when I lived in Berkeley, because everybody was. I didn't have to be one anymore.

> I had to keep flipping back the pages to my earlier list to do the arranging. After a while, I realized that flipping back is a waste of energy. Then I thought about all the times I "flip back" to the past in my mind, and what a waste of energy that is. I want to stop doing that.

> The seeds of who I've become and who I'm becoming were always there—but obscured by a lot of negative garbage, along with inconsequential garbage that was put there by the culture I grew up in. So, although it's been a long haul, I can see that the seeds of my becoming are there from the start.

ARRANGING BY HOPE

Arranging according to *hope* is the third approach to arranging. Although it is the most unusual, it is often the most helpful. Because of the deeper concentration involved in arranging by *hope*, this method is the only one that calls for a full fifteen minutes—and not a minute less. Set a timer, a stopwatch, or an alarm clock.

<u>Hope destroyed</u> [names include *Procrastinator, Liar-Liar, Olive Oyl*]:

If you don't move, you die. Tomorrow is now, to think about it now is important. Olive Oyl ends the list in her gangly chalk-on-blackboard voice:

Pay attention! she says. Move without pause, your stillness will be how a river becomes still, the surface reflecting and gleaming and the motion beneath ongoing, incessant, a dance toward the source....

<u>Hope created</u> [names include *Truth-sayer, Smiling Wall, Judge, Musician, Artist, Friend, Swimmer, Healer, Tom Terrific*]:

I look forward to life and its music, the rhythm that moves my body, each of its cells, each of its spaces between the cells. My name is Sara and I am daughter, sister, mother, lover, woman-spirit. I can lead other women. I have my masculine side as well—*Tom Terrific*. I am in a perfect life to be both man and woman. I speak fully and listen fully. I do not fill the spaces with dreams or fears. I am clear. I am expressive. I move. I am the river and the dark women drumming the river. I am the river and I swim the river. I am the river and I pollinate the Indian Paintbrush dotting the banks. I am loved deeply. I love deeply, as deep as the place in this river where the current races its strongest self.

Arranging and patterning by hope, while always illuminating, sometimes brings painful insights. Todd, a high school senior, tells us that his list surprises him: "All the names that create hope are names I've given myself and have known all my life. All those on the 'destroy hope' list were names given to me by other people—including my friends."

We look at him. That's a lot of sudden insight for someone his age. "It's okay," he says. "I probably knew it all along but didn't want to know. It's hard to admit, but it's time for me to make new friends."

PATTERNING "OUTSIDE THE BOX"

Because we are working with lists, and therefore with words, patterning usually focuses on word arrangements. We analyze our lists to see which words are on the top or the bottom, on the right or the left. But often we do our best patterning when we bypass our normal modes of thinking altogether, stretching our imaginations and looking at the whole instead of the parts.

When you get out of your head and pattern more creatively, great surprises await you—as the next two stories will show.

The Blonde Bombshell

Lois says that *the blonde bombshell* was one of her nicknames. That's who she had been when she was younger—although "often with extra sand in the hourglass." I think she looks terrific as she is, but I keep my thoughts to myself.

We arrange our names by duration, then move into patterning. People share insights:

> "My positive names are all of longer duration than the negatives."
> "Names I gave myself show the major turning points in my life."

Lois raises her hand, excited. The usual ways of patterning don't work for her, she says. She then reminds me that I also suggested "soft-focusing" (that is, looking at your list as if you've just had your eyes dilated). So she tried it.

"I looked down, and there before me, in bright pink ink, were all my names 'arranged' into a blonde bombshell—and this time with just the right amount of sand in the hourglass!"

She holds up her list to show us. There she is—the blonde bombshell. No other form of patterning could have returned that image to her present self. We laugh, we cheer, and Lois wipes her eyes.

I have no way of explaining how the words on her arranged list happened to form that perfect hourglass. All I know is that when we pattern creatively, we always get the answers we need. A few years later, Lois sends me her workshop notes.

"Six months later," she adds, "I started developing a piece called *Body Language*, which is a spoken-word rap of every name everyone has given to my body. At some point, I know it will end up being part of a performance piece around body image and self-acceptance." As a writer and a comedienne, she says, she has discovered that "the most important work is deeply playful."

I couldn't agree more. As Jung said, the mediator between the spiritual and the material is always the imagination. Certainly for *naming*, *arranging*, and *patterning*, the more relaxed and playful the work, the deeper the insights.

The Tree

Looking awe-struck, Mary tells us she got a tree.

"You arranged your names like a tree?"

"No, the names arranged themselves like a tree. Look—"

She holds up her list of names, arranged by duration. Like Lois's blonde bombshell, they create a distinct visual pattern—in Mary's case, the image of a tall leafy tree. A column of fourteen single names forms the trunk. The others leaf out—from three words immediately above the trunk to as many as six across in the middle lines, ending with three across and then one on top—to form a beautiful tree.

Had Mary looked solely at the words, rather than at shape and outline, she would have missed the pattern and missed its message. Looking at the trunk, Mary says, she now knows what supports and nourishes her.

CONTINUING TO PATTERN

Once you've begun patterning, you may never stop. Months and even years after each workshop, I receive emails and letters from people, telling me what they're still discovering in their lists—and about themselves. As one person wrote:

> I realized that the names for myself that were descriptors of my artist soul created hope in me. They still felt somewhat "put on" at that point, yet they did create hope. This insight was the beginning of growing into an ability to more fully accept this artist part of myself.
>
> I now know that being an artist has nothing to do with "doing art" or creating anything. It relates to who I am, at a core place inside, how I view the world. Separating the doing-ness from the being-ness has been a big part of my journey [since the workshop]. Not surprisingly, the old work titles that even then felt "outdated, restrictive, too narrow, and too prescriptive" are dropping away, as I find myself attracted to other work.

NAMING, ARRANGING, AND PATTERNING AS A DAILY PRACTICE

Naming, arranging, and patterning—when you wisely and often use it—will bring you into closer contact with your soul. It is the first and most basic step for every spiritual alchemist. All you have to do is name, arrange, and pattern, especially at every turning point of your life. By doing the work yourself, rather than turning your questions over to someone or something else, you are the one in charge of your own life. You are becoming your own alchemist.

When I say "something" or "someone" else, I mean everything and everyone from clergy and psychotherapists to Tarot cards, the I Ching, or local intuitive readers. I say this while having great respect for both psychotherapy and intuitive counseling, in the hands of skilled and compassionate practitioners. Great insights and growth often arise from a therapeutic relationship. If you are in such a relationship, your becoming a spiritual alchemist will actually enhance and accelerate the process.

But the problem I see in too many people is that they hand over their inner power to the therapist, the psychic, or the Tarot cards. They still believe that the answers to their deepest questions are *out there*, not *within themselves*. They are consequently—and mistakenly—attributing the power of their higher consciousness to somebody or something else.

When you consciously choose to name, arrange, and pattern, you are doing two important things at once: keeping your own intuitive power *and* increasing your own self-awareness.

For example, let's say that you need more time alone but find yourself in a web of too many social obligations. Part of the problem is that you have good relationships with a lot of people, many of whom want to spend time with you. To find your solution to this problem, make a list of everyone who wants your time—and arrange it according to *hope*: Which of these names create hope, and which destroy hope? Which of these names energize you, and which make you tired just thinking about them? You'll know very quickly which "friends" to drop. (While the patterning doesn't suggest that these people are harmful, it alerts you that you need to create a better balance between alone time and people time. It also shows you which people have the highest *positive* priority in your life.)

As long as you're willing to be creative, you can use naming, arranging, and patterning to help you solve any problem you have. For everything from when to hold an important business meeting to how to gracefully get out of an awkward situation, from deciding on a college major to understanding why you're deathly afraid of being alone in the dark, naming, arranging, and patterning will give you your best and wisest answers.

Duration, in particular, is highly adaptable to a great many situations. Let's say you're thinking about changing jobs or professions. For each job or profession—the one you have now and the one you're contemplating—make a list of pros and cons. Then consider the three types of arranging. *Chronology* clearly won't help, because the contemplated job or profession is in the future. Arranging by *hope* won't work, because the pros and cons already cover "creates" or "destroys" *hope*. By process of elimination, that leaves *duration*—but how can you apply duration to a job you've never had?

This is where you become creative: Convert *duration of time* into, say, *intensity of feelings*. Rather than considering which qualities, attitudes, and feelings have *longer duration*, ask which have *greater intensity*. Arrange the lists for each job by *intensity*, start patterning, and you'll have your answer.

If *intensity of feelings* doesn't work for you, then think of the quality you value the most, the quality you most wish to live by. Integrity? Honesty? Service? Humility? Passion? (Notice that we're back to *naming* again.) Once you can name the quality, then create a scale of 1–5 or 1–10 and arrange the pros and cons according to *intensity of fulfilling* [the quality you chose]. Either way, once you do the arranging and patterning, you'll have your answer.

However, you can apply the practice of naming, arranging, and patterning in even more creative ways, as you'll see in the next exercise. Working with your names was only the warm-up! ⚡

Knowing Your Beliefs

This second exercise in *Naming*, *Arranging*, and *Patterning* will give you practice with another, even more useful way of applying the technique. The exercise will bring you closer to being able to hear the voice of your own soul, thereby taking you deeper into alchemy.

This chapter contains the naming exercise and a two-part arranging exercise. Only after you have done these in sequence—and have read the rest of the chapter—will you be properly prepared to do the patterning.

EXERCISE 2

Naming Your Beliefs

Naming Your Beliefs

5 minutes

1. List all of your beliefs about yourself, beliefs that you hold now, today. (Although Exercise 1A included names from the past, this exercise focuses you completely on what you believe at the present moment.)

> *Helpful Hint*
>
> If you're not certain what you "believe" about yourself, ask yourself:
> "What kind of a person am I?"
> or
> "What words would I use to honestly describe myself?"

2. Keep your answers straightforward and direct, not wildly complicated.

3. Write down your answers in single words, short phrases, or whole sentences. If you find yourself about to write long philosophical answers, limit yourself to simple adjectives.

4. When you are finished, turn the page.

NAMING BELIEFS

While your previous list of names was composed mostly of nouns, this list may be mostly adjectives: friendly, thoughtful, selfish, talkative, private, conscientious, spiritual...? The previous list included other people's names for and ideas about you, past and present. But this list is yours, for you, as you feel about yourself today.

ARRANGING YOUR BELIEFS

This time, you are not arranging by duration, chronology, or hope. This new two-part method of arranging is completely different. The first part, as you've already discovered, involves what psychologists call *free association*. It means that the moment you hear Word A, you name the first Word B that pops into your head, without thinking about it. (It's easy: I say *hot*, you say *cold*. I say *up*, you say *down*. I say *banana*, you say...?) In this process, the less you think and the more you play, the better the results.

When you free associate every item on your list of beliefs into some kind of furnishing, you can use anything that can go inside four walls. I don't mean just tables, chairs, and sofas—what we think of as furniture—but also exercise machines, knick-knacks, doorstops, windows, dishes, towels, books, toys, jewelry.... In other words, anything that can go inside—or be part of—four walls. No redwood trees or mountain lakes.

"Nothing living?" some people ask.

"Well, houseplants are living, aren't they? You can use *anything*—with the emphasis on *thing*—that can go in a building, in a room, inside a structure. But don't bother imagining a structure. Just let the furnishings themselves pop into your head."

This part of the workshop brings up the most questions. I don't tell anyone until afterwards that one man actually had an indoor swimming pool as one of his furnishings. I want everyone to make up his or her own.

Occasionally, somebody feels stymied and begs for examples. I keep it simple: "How about taking *nice* and turn it into a heating pad? a cookie? Whatever pops into your mind."

It's best to do the work as quickly as you can. If you get stuck on a word, skip it and go on to the next one. (You'll come back to the word later.) The first word that comes to your mind is the right one—not necessarily the "right one" for always but the right one for now. If you find your mind freezing, so that you can't think of anything, close your eyes and let an image of something appear in your mind's eye. If that doesn't work, then look around the room you're sitting in, count to five, and whatever object you happen to be looking at when you say five is "it."

Once you get started, you'll probably have fun—good, playful fun. The only people who struggle are those who ask too much of themselves. People who can't let themselves go out to play. People who used to stay in during recess doing their homework. People who have put game playing behind them, because they think that being a grown-up is serious business. If you're one of those people (I know them well, because I used to be one), just use the counting-to-five technique, and you'll start to loosen up. Maybe by the time you're done with this book, you won't be "one of those people" anymore.

Part of learning to be a spiritual alchemist is to let go of the illusion of perfection. As I mentioned earlier, we are here to learn to be human, not to learn to be perfect. Authentic spiritual alchemists know better than to take themselves so seriously that they forget to have fun. Spiritual alchemists know how to laugh—and especially at themselves.

If you're giving this book a quick read-through before doing the exercises, I urge you to do Exercises 2, 2A, and 2B now, before continuing. Otherwise, the rest of this chapter—and the powerful work that follows—may not only not make sense to you but also get in the way of your process. Take the time now—you'll be glad you did.

DISCUSSING THE FURNITURE

People always have lots of questions about their furniture:

"Why is my *unique* a piano?"
"I don't understand why I have five table lamps but no tables."
"Why did I make *helpful* a pair of high-heeled shoes when I hate wearing heels?"

With "why" questions about things like the *unique* piano, I tell everyone to wait until we get to the second part of the arranging phase. For the five table lamps without a table, I (or someone else) might say anything from "maybe you need a lot of light on the ground floor of something in your life" to "you'll find out soon enough...."

Some questions spark good-natured laughter, with everyone tossing answers back and forth:

"Why does his dictionary mean *smart* while mine means *overwhelmed*?"
"Why should your dictionary be like his? You don't look like him!"
"Of course your dictionary was overwhelming. It's got so many words in it, and you're a teacher, you're supposed to know them all...."
"Why did I have trouble finding something for *picky* when I had no trouble finding furniture for everything else?"
"Well, you're just being picky about *picky*—that fits!"

For beliefs that people wish to get rid of, wastebaskets, trash containers, dustbins, and toilets are common symbols. Although bed is a common choice for *passionate, sexual,* or *sensual,* other symbols show up, from fireplace ("I'm smokin'!") to sofa. Creativity runs wild, because no two people are the same. Just as no two sets of fingerprints are alike, no two sets of symbols are alike. People's dreams are as individual as the dreamer. For all that we are microcosms of a larger reality, we are nonetheless unique ones.

MEANINGS OF MEANINGS...

Sometimes half the fun is listening to other people present their "furniture." Not surprisingly, most furnishings have obvious meanings. When *angry* appears as a butcher's knife or *anxious* shows up as a psychiatrist's couch, everyone laughs appreciatively at the appropriateness of the symbol. Because the unconscious mind is often highly literal, some items are outright puns:

- "**throw** rug" (angry)
- "**hope** chest" (hopeful)
- "table **runner**" (energetic)
- "photographic paper" (free to **develop**)
- "**spyglass**" (curious/nosy)
- "a wrapped **present**" (gifted)

Other furnishings, while not technically puns, have rich associative meanings:

- "light switch dimmer" (still too demanding): behavior needs *dimming*
- "Stradivarius" (finely tuned): *fine* instrument that needs *tuning*
- "picture window" (enlightening): lets in *light, shows the big picture*
- "rock" (obstinate): as in *rock solid, rock bottom, hard as a rock*
- "lightning rod" (transforming): the rod *transforms* energy
- "fireplace" (trying to release arrogance) and chimney (trying to stop being judgmental): *burning it up*, seeing it *go up in smoke*
- "bed with comforter" (eases my grief): *comforts me*
- "a lone cupboard door" (I am hidden): being *"in the closet"*

Other associations are equally clear: "no locks" for *trusting,* "windows" for *open,* or "books" for *well-educated.* But some furnishings make sense only after we really stretch our imaginations or get an explanation from the decorator:

- medicine cabinet for *sad*:
    "A medicine cabinet can contain 'downers.'"
- books for *sometimes scattered*:
    "I sometimes have books scattered all over the house."
- eyeglasses for *forgetful*:
    "I always forget where I left my glasses."

But not all furnishings have obvious meanings, even for the person who came up with them. Hearing that an oil painting represents "I am shunned" or that heavy drapes stand for "spasmodically artistic," everyone gets curious: why a painting? why drapes?

As often as not, the response is "I don't know. That's what I got." But sometimes the answers are as revealing as they are fascinating:

> *Chandelier* represents my belief that my soul is eternal, because it hangs up high, above everything, powered by a source above. So it is connected to a higher power.

When participants ask a question about their own furniture, the question itself often contains the answer. For example, Irene is an immigrant who has lost much of her accent over 46 years in the States. But she still identifies with her home country. She tells us that she understands all of her furnishings except the curtains. "I have curtains for *adjusting*. Why did I put curtains? I don't like curtains."

"That's easy," someone says. "You put curtains for adjusting because you don't like curtains and you don't like adjusting!"

Irene giggles and puts a hand over her mouth. Her choice of furnishing has revealed a truth she's been denying for years. But now, in the form of curtains, the truth shines with humor, and she can accept it.

SELF-DECEPTION

We can be only as honest about our beliefs as we are clear-eyed in facing ourselves. Some of us, in our human frailty, want to view ourselves only in the most positive light. The concept of soul work often attracts people who wish to see themselves as being perfectly spiritual: always on the "right" path, always having the "right" thoughts. Not surprisingly, their furnishings stand for qualities quite different from the ones they display in the workshop. On occasion, such self-deception appears almost comic. Most of the time, however, the other participants find it disturbing.

A Caucasian couple in their mid-thirties comes to the workshop, holding hands and making eyes at each other. She is an energetic, smartly dressed corporate professional. He wears long hair in a ponytail and a necklace with a symbol from an Asian religion. Soft-spoken, he talks earnestly about his spiritual journey. All of his beliefs about himself are loving, gentle, kind, and so on. *Tender* is a wall-to-wall carpet, he says, because tenderness underlies everything he does.

But it turns out that he registered for the workshop only when he discovered that his girlfriend was planning to come without him. When she speaks, he watches her like a hawk. When anyone says something with which he disagrees, his face tightens and reddens, and his body stiffens. His "tender" expression disappears as he attacks my point of view with visible hostility. He walks out at the break without saying good-bye, insisting that she accompany him. We are sorry for her that she does.

After they leave, someone mutters, "Well, if he's tender, I'm the Queen of England." Another person adds, "I was married to someone like him once—emphasis on *was*." For all his talk of being tender, he fooled no one but himself...and possibly his girlfriend.

To become spiritual alchemists, to do deep spiritual work—whether by naming, arranging, and patterning or by any other means—we have to be honest about who we are. The more I do this work, the more strongly I believe that our emotional development determines the level of our spiritual development. In other words, if I am emotionally still an adolescent, then how adult can I be spiritually? If I am deceiving myself about, say, my "tenderness," then how can I have an authentic relationship with my soul? How can I get any value out of spiritual messages I receive if I am not yet adult enough to understand, accept, and apply them?

We have to develop emotional honesty if we are going to have a genuine relationship with our soul. We cannot listen to its voice at its purest pitch if our emotional immaturity creates static interference. So if your list contained any negatives at all, good for you. You're being honest with yourself. On the other hand, if your list contained all negatives, that's another story. That's not "being honest," that's being too hard on yourself. That's somebody else's voice talking. As you continue with the exercises, you'll soon discover your good qualities—and how many of them you have.

CREATING YOUR ROOM

The second part of arranging your beliefs was to put them all under one roof, that is, all in one room, on one piece of paper, so that you can easily visualize its layout. If you haven't done this yet, turn to p. 43 and follow the instructions. If you've already created your room, continue reading.

The room you've just designed can be any shape or size. You may have made it square, rectangular, circular. It may look strange and exotic or ordinary and boring. You may have modeled it on a room in your house, with the same number of doors and windows. It may be an attic, a basement, or a space ship. It doesn't matter. Your room, at this point, is still in the design stage. It's an architect's preliminary sketch, not a finished product.

Some people's rooms serve all the functions of a home, with a kitchen in one corner, a desk and computer in another, and a bedroom near a fireplace. Others have brooks running through their rooms. (Mine, once totally unimaginative, now has an observatory roof.) You may have made it a huge space, with dividers separating what otherwise would be rooms. You may have two stories, a porch, a balcony, a skylight, or wall-to-wall carpeting in your favorite color. You may also, like one person I remember, have a very large toilet that you've had to hide behind a sofa or a ceiling-high potted plant.

"But why a room?" some people ask. "Why are our beliefs indoors, inside walls?"

As I said in the introductory chapter, I don't believe that we can reach the voice of our own soul from outside of ourselves. Instead, from *within* the selves that we are, we can commune with everything from the natural world to the divine. From within the essence of who you are, you communicate with your soul—not from somewhere outside it. Remember: as above, so below. Who we are, from the inside out, determines not only our ability to connect with the divine but also the quality of that connection.

This room, as it eventually unfolds, represents you in your human form—your boundaries, your limits, your separateness. Just as your body houses your spirit, your room houses all of your qualities—the best and worst of you as you experience yourself at this moment.

As I also said, I am a Jew, raised in a tradition that teaches us to look inside ourselves for spirit. One of our well-known sages, the Kotzker Rebbe, once pointed to verse 25:8 in Exodus, which reads: V*e'asu li miqdash veshakhanti betokham* ("Let them make me a sanctuary that I may dwell among them"). Noting that the Hebrew text read "among them" and not "within it," he taught that the real sanctuary was an inner structure. For the "Blessed Holy One" to dwell among them, he said, people must build a sanctuary in their hearts.

This room that you have begun constructing is soon to become that sanctuary, the place where you and your soul can meet. It doesn't have to look spiritual—and it certainly doesn't have to look like what you think of as an inner sanctum or a laboratory. Let your imagination continue doing the work, because, as Jung observed, the imagination is where the real work takes place.

MAKING THE ROOM

How you actually make your room—whether by drawing little boxes or making a piece of art—is up to you. The method you use doesn't matter (unless you are a visual artist, because then everything you create matters). The purpose of the drawing is to help you visually focus during your patterning work. *Seeing* your room, as opposed to thinking about it, is what makes the patterning process work.

Yet some people find that the actual process of art-making becomes part of what they learn from their room. For example, poet Robin Chapman has a room containing "some old piles of old messes, unneeded now, and the new piles of creativity at work... connected to artists in the world." She writes in her notebook:

> What do I learn from making the room with bright-colored scraps? Use everything, nothing left out. You can be both intertwined and whole. Old relationships are not failures, but contain life energy.

Are they *opposite* one another?

Are they *clustered together* or *separate from* the others, in one corner of the room?

3. Notice their relationship in terms of scale: Is one of them much *larger* or *smaller* than the other?

4. Notice their "feeling" relationship to one another: Is one *hiding* the other? *smothering* the other? *dominating* the other?

5. Choose the word or phrase that best describes the relationship.

> *Helpful Hint*
>
> Only you can know what the relationship is. If you think that somebody else might look at your drawing and say "the chair is on the rug," but you see the rug as supporting the chair, then "supporting" is the right patterning relationship. Trust yourself completely while doing the patterning.

6. Write down the relationship you see between the two items you selected.

7. Look at your list of beliefs to see what belief each item represents.

8. Now apply the relationship between the two items to the two beliefs.

> *Helpful Hint*
>
> You may find that the patterning work is easier or goes faster if you write down the appropriate belief next to each item in your room. (Some people like to see the beliefs in the room, but other people don't. Follow your preference.)

9. Now that you are done patterning those two items, go around your entire room, looking for relationships between and among all objects. Pay attention to any relationships that immediately catch your eye. Remember, the relationship between the items will be the same as the real relationship between the beliefs they represent.

10. Write down all relationships as soon as you notice them.

11. Keep going around the room, looking at the relationships between objects, and discovering new things about yourself.

12. Try bypassing ordinary ways of looking. Let the patterns leap off the page at you. Let the relationships surprise you.

13. Every time you make a discovery, remember to write it down.

When you have finished patterning, continue reading.

PATTERNING THE ROOM

Patterning the room is simple, enlightening, and often playful. Let's first review the steps in greater detail: Randomly choose any two items in the room you drew, and look at them. Then relate the items to one another in terms of their spatial relationship: Is A on top of B? Is B supporting A? Are they touching? Does A hang over B? Is B below or under A?

In other words, using primarily prepositions (over, under, by, near, across from, on top of, behind, in front of) and "-ing" verbs (facing, hiding, covering), find the relationship between the objects. Then transfer that relationship to the quality that the item represents.

For example, you may have a coffee mug (*self-nurturing*) on a table (*stubborn*). If you see the table as *supporting* the coffee mug, then your stubbornness is *supporting* your self-nurturing. If you see the coffee mug as *resting on* the table, then your self-nurturing capabilities *rest on* your stubbornness. Either way, because the two are in some kind of contact, they are in some kind of relationship. More important, the relationship you see between the two items is the relationship you unconsciously see between the two qualities.

After you have patterned the first two items, go around the room and discover all the relationships. Here are a few examples of questions you might ask:

Why are those three items clustered together in one corner?

Why is the upper left-hand quadrant empty?

Why is a potted plant in the center of the room?

Why is the yo-yo in front of the sofa? Or is the yo-yo at the foot of the sofa? Or does the sofa loom over the yo-yo?

Does the end table support the table lamp, or does the lamp "shed light on" the table?

MORE PATTERNING TECHNIQUES

Over the years, creative participants have taught me other patterning techniques:

Size or *Scale:* Why is the *stubborn* table so big, compared to the tiny *self-nurturing* coffee mug? What important quality does the sofa represent, that it's so much larger than the yo-yo? If your *hospitality* dwarfs your *creativity*, you are probably telling yourself that you need to spend less time on house guests and more time on your poems or your pottery.

Color: Why are these five items red, but not any others? Why are those central items bright, while the ones by the stove are pastel? Do the bright colors make you happy, or do they take over the room?

Shape: Why are those three items sharp and spiky, while everything else in the room is soft and fluffy? Is spiky a good thing (that is, do you need some "spice" or sharpness in the middle of a Cream-of-Wheat life)?

What does my *doubtful* wall-to-wall rug say about my image of myself as self-confident?

Finding the answers to such questions lies at the heart of spiritual alchemy—and is therefore a natural part of the process. That's why I've peppered the book with generous samplings of examples from workshop participants. The more you learn from their experiences, the broader your understanding of the process grows, and the better you can pattern, understand, and eventually work incredibly well in your room. Meanwhile, if you still think you need help with the patterning, that's what friends are for. Take your patterning questions to your closest friend and talk them over. Often you'll discover that asking the questions aloud will give you your answers before your friend has time to reply.

A good example of the power of sharing your patterning comes from a friend, after I suggested that she reposition her furniture. She later wrote that patterning her room was the "most intense" part of the workshop for her:

> The room proved to be very important to me, because within it was a comfortable chair. I identified this chair as being my survivorship from childhood sexual abuse. I also said that it was a part of the foundation that informed all that I did in my life.
>
> Your response was to ask me if I could move the chair away from the center of the room. You asked me if I could find a new foundation for my life. You suggested that letting my survivorship continue to inform everything in my life was hindering my growth on other levels…, that my survivorship was a part of my past. And although it was a fact in my life, it did not have to inform everything I did currently or in the future.
>
> That was something I really had not considered so closely until you said it to me. Spirit has been sending me signals to stop dwelling in the past, to live more for now, but your saying this to me was the most direct.

In the same letter, she continues: "How does one let go of something that was a central part of one's life for years? I am working to find out."

My friend wasn't asking me for answers but rather relating a question she had posed for herself. By going to her room and using it as her laboratory, and by being open to observations from others *if the observations fit*, she was committing herself to the process of spiritual alchemy.

And so will you, as you continue the exercises. Perhaps the greatest value of patterning in your inner laboratory is that you can find the answers to your most pressing questions—or your true path to those answers. Through working with your soul voice, you get the answers straight from your soul.

But before you can "go to your room" to ask questions, you need to consider as many ways of patterning a room as possible. You'll then be able to get the most value out of the exercise—and the most insight out of your room.

OTHER WAYS OF FINDING PATTERNS

Because our rooms are as unique as we are, no two sets of items or patterns are alike. A sofa in the corner of one person's room may be *lazy*, while a sofa in the middle of another person's may be *sexual*. Perhaps the person with the lazy sofa doesn't have sex on her couch, or perhaps he isn't sexual. Perhaps the person with the sexual sofa doesn't have a bed in his room, or perhaps she.... The possibilities are endless.

Some patterning, as you probably discovered when choosing your furnishings, involves unconscious punning. For example, one young man wrote: "No chairs. I don't need to sit. I can now stand on my own two feet." Another person observed that her *talkative* nature was clustered in one corner with *kindness* and *compassion*. This pattern told her that her talkativeness, instead of being self-centered, was "a kind, compassionate engagement with people."

Here are some other patterning comments, to give you more ideas about the way people pattern, and to expand your understanding of the process:

I can get to self-restoration (attic) only through complexity (staircase to attic)—no easy route.

The helpless swimming pool has a slimming lounge chair next to it. I feel (or felt) helpless to lose the weight that settled on me like a parasite. The caring orthopedic gravity boots hang near the helpless pool. I feel helpless to help those I care for.

Integrated = windows evenly spaced; open = big picture windows; discerning = smaller windows. Integrity is like a mandala, even with different-sized windows. No matter which window I look out from, or in what direction I look, I bring all of myself with me.

I am not good at breaking into cliques is a round sofa, only partly in the room, and the rug (*I am attractive*) is on the floor in front of it. People find me attractive and I find them attractive, but it is hard for that rug to fit with that sofa. It doesn't belong there.

What about *your* room? As you read, if more patterning thoughts about your room occur to you, be sure to write them down.

Other uses of basic patterning

Beyond its obvious uses in clarifying the room, patterning serves two other powerful purposes. One is to send you off on an inner quest, to know yourself better. The other is to put you more deeply in touch with your authentic emotional self.

Starting a Quest

Veronica, for whom transformational work is very new, does clear, straightforward patterning. She presents her list of qualities first, so that her patterning notes make sense. These notes contain both comments and questions.

Selfish / sofa	Neat / lamp	Ugly / mirror
Organized / bookcase	Colorful / picture	Impatient / radio
Quiet / candle	Reflective / incense	Weak / exerciser
Lazy / easy chair	Undisciplined / rug	Tired / bed
Obsessive / TV	Growing / window	

"This was good for me," Veronica says, "because normally I would spend a lot of time intellectualizing."

Veronica's Patterning:
- My window (growing) is next to the bookcase (organized) in the corner; they are near each other but not touching. Why?
- On the organized bookcase is quiet and reflective. I need organization in order to have these qualities in my life. The window stands for growth. The window is very big because I have a lot of growing to do.
- The radio (impatience) is on top of the TV (obsessive). My impatience comes from being obsessive. These are just above the exerciser, which represents weakness. Am I impatient and obsessive because I am weak? I like weakness in the corner.
- The bed is next to the mirror. I am tired and ugly. These are in a corner of my room. The mirror is small because deep down I can see beauty in me.
- The sofa in the middle stands for selfish. Why is selfish in the middle? Because I need to be selfish, in the way of caring for myself before anything else can happen. This selfishness is a good type of selfishness.
- My picture (colorful) is back against the wall, seemingly all by itself. It's also small. Why?

Veronica's recurrent "why?" is typical of first-time patterners. Seeing something new, she wants to understand it. Her room, through patterning, starts her on an inner journey, spurring her to delve more deeply into her beliefs and motivations. She is already on her way to a more profound knowing of self.

Understanding Feelings

Patterning also helps us clarify why certain emotions are recurrent in our lives. By so clearly showing us how these feelings connect to our actions and desires, patterning can give us the same rich insights we might get from a session with a therapist.

Liza's room helps her understand how anger and determination are related in her current situation. Betrayed by two men shortly after her grandfather's death, she has stronger feelings than she had been willing to admit to herself. Her items include:

obstinate about integrity	rock
still angry about men	throw rug
healthy	sacred well
increasingly confident	bucket in well
successful	rope holding bucket
determined to meet goals	grandfather's photo
strong	big boots
boundaries	door

As she starts to pattern, Liza discovers a big Freudian slip: Instead of writing the words "throw rug" next to "still angry at men," as she intended, she has written "*throw rock*"!

Her patterning notes are revealing:

- I have two rocks, one for being stubborn about my integrity and the other—the one I want to throw!!!—for being angry at men. I'm obviously very set on punishing those SOBs....
- The boots are between the "throw rock/rug" and my door. This means that my strength is what links my boundaries and my anger. Because I have boundaries, I can be strong in expressing my anger.
- I'm using the rock of "obstinate about integrity" as a doorstop. It helps me focus the anger.
- My grandfather's photograph, which stands for "determined," is very big. He was always determined, and now I am taking on his qualities.
- The "successful" rope on the "increasingly confident" bucket allows me to draw good health from the sacred well.

Patterning possibilities are infinite. For every pattern that you might see, somebody else might find another. For example, Liza sees her strength as "linking" her boundaries and her anger, because that's how she feels. Somebody else with the same three symbols might see the strength as separating her boundaries and her anger, and say, "Because my inner strength allows me to have boundaries, it frees me from my anger. As a boundaried person, I don't need to be angry anymore."

But Liza is Liza, not somebody else. The interpretation is hers to make. While well-intentioned friends and family may make suggestions to you, just as workshop participants offer interpretations to people explaining their rooms, only you can interpret your symbols. Only you can know what you feel—and certainly only you can know what you believe about yourself.

TRUST YOURSELF

The problem for many of us is that we live in a culture that promotes getting outside help and going to "experts" for inner answers. As the old saying goes, "An expert is an ordinary person who lives at least 50 miles away." But you, only you, are the expert in your own life. You—and no one else—have the clearest, straightest, most direct access to the voice of your own soul.

Because you are part of your soul, you can easily connect with it. Just as a carpenter comes to a job with the right tools, you too will come away from this process with the tools for making your laboratory an access point for your own true answers. A vibrant, creative, restful space, where real alchemy can take place.

Your inner laboratory is just beginning to take shape. As you do the next exercise and read the next chapter, you will delve deeper into its richness and explore it further. ⚗

CHAPTER
4

Exploring Your Laboratory

A t this point, what will become your laboratory is still functioning like a crucible—the open vessel in which transformation takes place through initial purification. Even though your laboratory will become the retort (a self-enclosed vessel), you are still at the stage of "purifying" who you have always thought yourself to be. As you pattern the room, you refine—and thus purify—your understanding of yourself.

Having completed Exercise 3, you may now feel that your patterning work is complete. Yet you may wish to explore your laboratory further, to take your refining process to a deeper level. Exercise 4 is therefore an optional exercise along the path of spiritual alchemy. For those of you wishing to hone your understanding of the patterning process, do Exercise 4 now. For those of you electing to skip Exercise 4, simply read it as part of the chapter. You may find that you want to do the exercise at another time.

EXERCISE 4

Exploring Your Laboratory

EXERCISE 4

Exploring Your Laboratory

 5 to 20 minutes

1. Return to your drawing and your patterning notes.

2. Study both until some new patterns become clear.

3. Referring to the items in your room as necessary, write a short paragraph or two describing the patterns. Write conversationally, as if you are emailing your closest friend or writing confidentially in a journal.

4. When you have finished the exercise, continue reading.

MORE PATTERNING

Betsy, an adopted woman whose list of names included "not supposed to be" and "illegitimate," finds the negatives in her room almost overwhelming: "I have no windows—no clarity, no beauty. The three smallest things in the room are the most positive, but they have a lot of large negatives to contend with: *discouraged chair, angry stove, tired bed, unhealthy refrigerator.* All the big stuff is sitting on my creativity (floral carpet), but all the good stuff is not connected to it." Her room, she tells us, "is cluttered with pain."

Despite the "large" negativity, Betsy feels hopeful:

> I couldn't do anything about the pain before, because I didn't understand its dynamics. Now that I see the *unhealthy* refrigerator, I know that eating better will make me emotionally healthier and physically stronger, so that I don't go to bed tired all the time. Best of all, underneath everything and supporting *me*, is my creative carpet. As long as creativity is my base, I can take care of the rest!

The more deeply you explore your room, the more intimately you know yourself. Describing your room is the first place to start your exploration. Once you can verbalize what you see, the patterns of the room's intricate structure become clearer. You begin to place yourself in the center of who you are and who you wish to become.

As we describe our rooms, honesty, insight, and awareness become our constant companions. Many of us see ourselves, for the first time, from both within and without. The "outside" perspective, surprisingly, is our old self-image; the inside view comes straight from the room, reflected in the patterns we find.

REVISITING NEGATIVE PERCEPTIONS

One of the core goals of the spiritual alchemist is to find a way to mediate the tensions between opposites. The process of turning lead into gold involved finding the key to turning something base into something pure. For the spiritual alchemist, the goal is to hold the tensions between the emotional and ethical opposites, such as good and evil or compassionate and punitive. An alchemist doesn't seek to eliminate the negative but to find a way of containing or balancing it.

Some people, while exploring their rooms, suddenly see their "perceived negatives" in a completely new light. Diana writes:

> I LOVE MY SPACE. The opening in the center of *story telling*—how marvelous. Across from the *asker of questions* (door knocker)—but some questions become *stiff and unyielding* (door)—but I love the door. Knockers

to let me know who is there. The *magician* (picture) is also part of the door. It's great—my door is *stiff and unyielding* because then I can be with me!

I love my hallway, too—it's *bitchy*. Bitchy bitchy bitchy—a small space cut off from everything. I'm containing it.

When I'm quiet I go into the drawers in the *debilitated* table with a computer that's *delightful*. (I'm trying to hide from feeling debilitated by the computer that would help me in my work.)

I have a toilet that makes me feel *competent*.

Wow—there are real reasons behind my perceived negative qualities— they are really positive needs!! Excitement pouring through my veins as the blood pulses and surges through. Write about women being **good**! The Room of the Self, creating the Sacred Space.

Never want to change this room! Really satisfied—and **safe**!!

Having suddenly discovered that her "perceived negative" qualities are truly positive, Diana is energized and excited. Rather than wanting to change her room, to get rid of the negatives, Diana is happy with who she discovers herself to be.

Another woman, Lillian, finds not only insight but also strength in weakness:

In the center is *aspiration*, in the form of music, performance, enter- tainment. Of course this is my present path. What is closest? The kitchen, which represents *helpful*—I see myself as mother there—that is where I'm helpful—or supposed to be, but it is blocked off by an inner wall. The furnace of *anger* is just below and icy *insecurity* is stored there. If the help is associated with motherhood/nurturing, it is corrupted by insecurity and anger. I am not helping my aspiration because of insecurity and anger. These of course are part of me as mother—I am insecure as a mom and angry because motherhood distracts me from my true aspiration. And, of course, anger and insecurity are inherited from my own mother.

Underneath it all is my *lack of focus* (basement), the foundation. It is under the whole room.

Upon entering, one sees the *aspiration* (CD player) with a candle (*hope*) behind it.

Most of the positive qualities are on the right (from the outside look- ing in): loving, kindness, growth, confidence. Negative qualities are on the left: fear, anger, insecurity, trite, disorganization. This world indicated my "male" side as strong, female side as flawed. However, from the inside looking out, the opposite is so. Is this the case—from the outside, I appear to be confident, loving, kind, growth-oriented, but inside I am fearful, trite, insecure...but also there is help here! Self-help, huh?

Lillian realizes that all the "self-help" she needs is already within her, in the form of her room. She can see herself as she wants to, as opposed to the way others might see her, because she is in control of her own perspective.

CLARIFYING CHANGE

One of the great values of patterning is to clarify what needs doing next. By patterning our rooms, many of us discover what we need to change—and how clear and simple that change really is. Here are two quite different examples:

> Even though I am smart and compassionate, these qualities are divided by my being irresponsible.... *Irresponsible* sits **between** *smart* and *compassionate*. If irresponsible were to go away, smart and compassionate could work together in my life.... Irresponsible also sits **opposite** passionate and changing.
>
> I can remove *irresponsible* from the room of my self since it's my room and I made it and I **TAKE RESPONSIBILITY!!!!!** This for me is the key to using the gifts of smart, compassionate, passionate, and changing for my soul's purpose.

> One of the insights I gained from the patterning exercise was: My ability to embrace change supports (1) my ability to translate complex ideas into meaningful bits of information for others, (2) living from my dreams, (3) living with imagination and creativity, and (4) living with purpose and vision.
>
> For me this is an encouraging insight which supports my going forward on my path. I have recently left my home city of 30-plus years; quit my job; and moved in with my partner, after having lived alone since my divorce 22 years ago. I see now how change is at the very center of who I am becoming.
>
> Another insight from the same exercise was: Living with Spirit as my guide supports living with a long-term perspective.

For both these individuals, change and choice are inseparable. In their different ways, they see change "at the center" of their life and their life purpose. The more they choose to change into the person they wish to become, the more central change becomes to their growth, and the more they allow it to guide their lives.

"Unconscious arrangement"

A psychotherapist on a spiritual path comes to the workshop. Elegant and poised, she exudes a natural self-confidence that feels genuine to everyone. She writes:

> Very unconscious "arrangement" in some ways—e.g., the closet with witch costume (*belief in magic—the real kind, miracles*) has a secret compartment for Hope Diamond (*I "treasure" my husband and son*). Putting the two together: First I thought the costume just belonged in a closet—then, when I put the Diamond there, I thought something so valuable should not be out in the open. Then I realized that I have thought of Jim and Scott as the two main **miracles** in my life—and both have brought *real* magic into it! (My unconscious at work.)

By using the word "unconscious" twice in one paragraph, she reveals that she hadn't expected to be surprised. As a good therapist, she knows herself well—consciously. The power of patterning the room, of course, is that it takes us past the conscious and into our deepest truths.

OPEN-ENDED QUESTIONS

In patterning your room, you may encounter questions you aren't ready to answer yet. If so, you're in the majority. These questions signal what you need to work on next and what intention you need to form. The Hebrew word for intention is *kavanah*, from the root "to aim," because forming an intention is like preparing to shoot an arrow or take a photograph. Just as concentration or focused intention is at the heart of alchemy, so too are questions.

Sharon asks, "Why are some bad things supported by strength?" The question is open-ended, rich with possibility.

Her observations:

- A curtain of *hatred* covers a *tender-hearted* window.
- The dominant feature: *desirability*, touched by *fat*? *Loving* and *insightful* complement *needy & fat*, almost like things to make them better.
- So much sits upon *strong*, including my altar (*spiritual*). Why is talented off to the side of *strong*? Why are some bad things supported by strength?
- The things that rest on the floor are loving, likable, WARM feelings— they are grounded. The things on walls, on others things, all are more air-oriented—they're in my head. That's why *talented* is on the floor. Funny, I **resisted** putting *sexual* and *liked* on the floor.

Sharon's honesty is the key to her self-discovery. By not hiding from uncomfortable questions, she sees that hatred is covering up or blocking off her tender heart, and that her talented self, though grounded, is not close enough to her strength. Because Sharon is willing to confront issues with her sexuality and the "bad things," her room will evolve into an inner laboratory that reflects her core integrity and desire to grow.

If you, like Sharon, have questions you can't yet answer, begin cultivating the discipline of not knowing. The power of the room is that it can contain all the "not knowing" for you until you are ready for the answer. The more you can allow yourself to "not know" all the answers to a growth-related question, the greater the chance that the answer will surface to greet you when you least expect it.

EFFECTS OF THE ROOM IN A GROUP SETTING

As we listen to one another present our rooms and share our insights, we grow, we change. Friends who knew each other before the workshop say, "I never knew you felt [this] or thought [that] about yourself." Strangers come closer, drawn to one another by the raw honesty that working with the room evokes.

I once worked with a small group of psychotherapists. They were so adept at processing emotions, from their years of professional experience, that all I had to do was turn them loose—and sit back and listen. One later wrote:

> I was just thinking of the process which develops qualities into objects, then places them in our "spaces." This was a very powerful process, and its graphic impact has stayed with me. I was also struck by the positive impact it had on the group process. I can still remember Joanne's intricately exquisite room and how it brought awarenesses to her that touched her sadness and, in turn, provoked such compassion in all of us.
>
> This is one memory, within a larger memory of a warm process among new and old friends, while outside the winter storm swirled....

Her beautiful evocation of group compassion among "new and old friends" shows the power of sharing your patterning insights with people you trust.

MAINTAINING ABSOLUTE PRIVACY

Some people love their rooms so much that they can't wait to invite people in. After all, they have a welcoming sofa, a passionate bed, a spiritual fireplace—and often a fully equipped kitchen. Why not have company?

But the room—your laboratory-to-be—is also a sacred room *of the self.* Of yourself, not anyone else's self. This room is composed of all your beliefs about yourself. Part of your uniqueness as a human being is that no matter how much you tell people who you are, what you believe, or what your history is, no one else can live in your skin. No one else will ever see you or experience you from the inside, the way you do.

Likewise, you can't crawl into the skin of any other human being. Love them and understand them as you may, you still can't see them one hundred percent from their perspective, as they see themselves. Understanding this truth is at the heart of spiritual alchemy, which involves balancing all opposites, including intimacy and aloneness.

Your room, therefore, is off limits to other people. Friends, family, lovers, spouses cannot come in—and do not need to. (Remember, they have their own room, just waiting to be created.) The problem is that the more exciting your room, the more you will probably want to share it.

But how can you share your room with others if you can't invite them in? You can have a telephone and call them from it. You can show people photos of the outside walls. You can send and receive email messages on your "relationship computer." You can have mail, along with the newspaper, delivered to your door. But the only person who can enter your room is you.

LONG-TERM EFFECTS OF PATTERNING THE ROOM

When a man in his 50s shows up on a Friday evening, straight from work in a suit and tie, I wonder what has led him to the workshop. With his impeccable attire and reserved manner, Bill shows no outward signs of being a spiritual seeker or an artist in search of inspiration.

Books and workshops with "spiritual" or "transformation" in their titles tend to attract fewer men than women. I suspect that the primary reason is cultural, along the lines of "real men don't eat quiche." Ever since the consciousness-raising meetings of the early 1970s, women have embraced the concept of transformation, for reasons both personal and financial. Over the following decades, major life transformations from housewife to older college student, from receptionist to project manager, from nurse to doctor, or from fully supported wife to single head of household with children have made women increasingly receptive to personal growth and spiritual awakenings. Whether inwardly motivated or outwardly imposed, transformational issues were in our faces. While some of us chose to change, many of us had no choice.

TRANSFORMING THE MALE

But for men, embracing transformation is doubly threatening. They have to give up illusions of superiority, societal mandates of what it means to "be a man," long-ingrained habits such as not crying when hurt. Transformation, for men, usually entails giving up their piece of the proverbial pie; and very few people with power—however hollow, superficial, or meaningless that power—ever want to relinquish it.

I always honor the presence of men—and so do almost all the other women. Occasionally a woman will feel stifled: "I can't say what I really feel, not with a man in here." But most women openly welcome the men, especially the kind who tend to show up: retirees seeking a spiritual awakening, college students with a spiritual bent, creative men who feel they have a book in them. As both their perspective on the world and the way in which they quest are different from ours, they contribute hugely to the process.

THE KNIGHT IN SHINING ARMOR

Bill doesn't fit any usual patterns. Soft-spoken, articulate, he keeps his private life to himself, saying simply that he's seeking to develop artistically and spiritually. Only when we begin describing our rooms do the rest of us discover the depth of him, the wealth of imagery, the profundity of his room. The *knight on his horse*, the *ideal woman* on horseback with him, the *bust of Aristotle*, the *cloud of mist*—none of these medieval, Arthurian images have come to any of us. Who is this man in pinstripes with such underlying romanticism? We pepper him with questions and draw him out.

Months later, I receive an email from him. We begin corresponding. He has cancer and is treating it holistically, without surgery or radiation. When I ask him if he will describe his room for this book, he sends back both a graph and his transformational story.

I leave his words intact, for you to see the very different style in which many men organize and present their insights, a difference that Bill's writing beautifully exemplifies. Even his understanding of the purpose of the exercise comes through a different filter, a different lens.

Bill writes:

> The goal of the exercise was to visualize a room containing objects that symbolized current personal attributes that could be expressed as an adjective. The idea was to objectify the disposition of the mind, body, soul, or place at this point in life.

STATUS AT TIME OF WORKSHOP – JULY 1999

I was a 56-year-old divorced white male; a project/program manager by day; a writer by night. I was coming out of an all-time low in my life. Four years earlier, I was diagnosed with a potentially lethal health condition, which I was treating naturally. Four months earlier, I ended a 24-year relationship with divorce. At the time of the workshop, I was beginning to find myself and get traction in my new life. I was in a period of self-reflection in which I had quit dating to do some deep inner work.

TRANSITIONAL PERIOD

After this workshop, I spent another four months in a self-imposed social isolation. In retrospect, this was one of the most empowering times of my life. I became much stronger and more independent, and refined my world view and self-concept.

In the fall of 1999, I felt this phase of my inner work was done, and became restless. It was time to reemerge. I synchronistically met and began dating a distinctive woman, another wandering mystic. I devoured books and workshops on many diverse subjects such as intuition, Jung, mind-body connections, Tarot, I-Ching, Taoism, Buddhism, Zen, holistic medicine. Along the way of my metamorphosis, I began to feel I had outgrown my professional life. By the turn of the year, I took leave from my secure, well-compensated, administrative officer position. By spring of 2001, I had resigned, despite an offer of a major promotion. This ended a long and highly diverse professional career. I traded income and security for freedom and life.

STATUS NOW – NOVEMBER 2001

I live modestly on a small pension. I have spent 2001 migrating back and forth between Madison where my two children and friends live, and Cleveland, where I assist in the care of my 90-year-old mother. In both locales, my days are active, full, and varied. Between assisting family members, I study and write extensively, exercise, jog, explore, meet people, and walk among the trees and streams that flow like my days. It might be interesting now to compare what the symbols precipitated by Natalie's workshop portended, with what transpired. And what dreams may come?

THE ROOM WITH A VIEW

My room contained the following "soul symbols." The associated adjectives and meanings are speculative and subject to interpretation. But they are what I seem to sense from them. For those of an astrological bent, I was born on the night of October ninth, nine minutes after nine.

Location	Symbol	Adjective	Meaning
Back Wall	A shadowy, disturbed male figure	Struggling, Conflicted	My tug of war between independence and intimacy.
Left Wall	A bust of Aristotle	Thinking	My rationalistic side.
"	A calculator	Quantitative, Analytical	My background in math and science.
"	A shelf of books	Academic	My eclectic interests and need to understand the totality of life.
"	A scale	Fair, Honest	My Libra tendencies toward balance, justice.
Right Wall	Knight on white horse. Arm is raised. Has a heart-like emblem on his chest.	Idealistic, Chivalrous, Helpful	My epically heroic side. Both yang-like hardness of warrior, with yin-like softness of humanitarian. Strength with tenderness.
"	Knight speaking	Instructive, Inspirational	My desire to help raise humanity through the transmission of ideals and ideas.
"	Lady with knight	Romantic	My fictional ideal love interest...to die for.
"	Dark clouds	Melancholy	My emergence from the "dark night of the soul" and strange attraction to this realm.
Lower Forward Wall	Body of still water	Warning, potentially threatening	My lake of mystery to transverse.
Middle Forward Wall	Cloud of mist ahead	Unknown, Mysterious	My sense of uncertainty, mystery, and radical, impending change. Spiritual, mystical, and transcendent themes.
Upper Lower Wall	Starry, Starry Night	Mystical, Transcendent	My priority and destiny: The eternal, ephemeral ascendance over the transient and material.
Overall structure/ style of room	Unadorned, basic, utilitarian, strong	Spartan	My style of encampment: simple, practical, strong, spiritually powerful.

A tiny woman in her 70s comes to the workshop at the annual week-long summer conference of the International Women's Writing Guild on the Skidmore College campus, and every day sits in the middle of the front row. Her eyes sparrow bright, she pays rapt attention, never saying a word. But after this "opposite" exercise, her hand shoots high in the air, waving like a flag in a windstorm. Her cheeks shine.

"My name is Virginia," she says, "and my word was Doughy."

"Doe-y??"

"D-O-U-G-H-Y," she spells. "Like dough." She turns an imaginary lump in her hands. "The word came immediately. I saw a mass of dough, slightly bigger than my two hands could comfortably hold. I didn't like it—not one bit! But there it was. Doughy. Then I thought, what would be the opposite of Doughy? What would 'fix' my situation? And immediately, Hard came. Maybe it's not exactly the opposite, but it's what I needed." She can hardly contain herself.

"I'm from North Carolina, and there's a poetry class I really want to enroll in, but the professor takes only ten students. My problem is that I'm here at Skidmore and registration at the university is this week. If I stay here all week, I won't be able to register. If I leave, I'll miss this wonderful experience. I know I could call, but I can't figure out the phones here. I didn't know what to do. So I asked Hard, and here's what he said":

She then reads aloud a clear set of instructions, telling her that she doesn't have a problem because all she has to do is learn to use the phone system on campus. "It's easy," says Hard. "You can do it—and if you can't, you can ask someone to show you how. Then you can call the professor and register." By now Virginia is almost jumping out of her chair. "I'm so excited! Doughy would never have thought of this." She glows, and we break into spontaneous applause.

The next day we ask for a report. Virgina giggles. "Well, I called yesterday, but when I got his recorded message, I was so flummoxed that I hung up without leaving a message."

"Did you ask Hard for help?"

"Yes! And he said, 'Don't be ridiculous. Why would you expect a professor to be in his office at four in the afternoon? Call the department office tomorrow morning and ask for his office hours. Call him then and explain your situation.'"

"And?"

"We had a pleasant chat, and I'm registered!!" We cheer. Someone suggests that she call on Hard as her ally, whenever she needs him. Virginia wonders how she "muddled through" so many years without him. I am fascinated by her personification of her qualities—not so much that Hard is male but rather that she has made both Doughy and Hard come alive. They are no longer just qualities; they are now real companions, living and breathing within her.

Virginia keeps in touch, sending me the poems she writes, along with the professor's comments and her A+ in his class. When I ask about the copy she promised me of Hard's focused instructions, she apologizes: "I misplaced my Skidmore folder with all the notes.... I'm sure it's here somewhere." In the margin she writes, "Typically Doughy!" Recalling how she had registered for her class within 24 hours of meeting Hard, she adds:

> I'm telling you, that was fast work for Doughy! In fact, Doughy would never have managed it. She would have been vaguely uncomfortable, felt vaguely guilty, and muddled through somehow.
>
> Such speedy action is/was unheard of for me. I think I am better now. And in class, it was so clear, so immediate. The name "Doughy" popped up as if a trap door had opened—and, just as magically, "Hard" appeared. And not just the word, but ways of acting!

Her professor, now a mentor, wants her to enter a book of poetry in a statewide contest. She's not sure she can meet the deadline.

"Ask Hard," I suggest. "Isn't he still around?"

"Oh, yes, he's here. At 77, I don't know what I'd do without him. But I hadn't thought to ask him about the contest. What a good idea!" She pauses. "It's fascinating. After being Doughy all my life, now Hard and Doughy are on equal footing. Instead of doing what I should do or what others want me to do, I do what I want. Time's too precious. Oh, what would I have done without Hard?"

SEEING THROUGH DIFFERENT EYES

This simple exercise of seeing through "opposite" eyes gives you practice with the important alchemical tool of seeing and feeling the opposites, not denying one in the service of the other. The other great benefit of this exercise is the discovery that what appears to be "opposite" may be so in ways you never expected. By discovering the true relationship between the qualities you have labeled as opposite, you come even closer to the self-knowing that lies at the core of spiritual alchemy.

Passing Through the Narrow Place

Judy is one of the sweetest people I've ever met. All she wants to do is write poetry and help others to help themselves. No one is surprised that her dominant quality is *heart*. Its opposite is *heartlessness*, and the minor tension is "my disorderly house."

You need to clear out: throw away, give away, get rid of...cut away the dead wood, divest yourself of those things that you no longer use that no longer serve your needs. You need to sort once and act quickly. You will not regret this purge. It will lighten and illuminate your inner space as well as your living space. It will make room for newness and creativity to enter. This will not be a loss, it will be an unfolding. It will be as if you were given the opportunity to start anew, bringing with you what you most need and cherish, leaving behind all that stifles and silences your inner voice. These are things you have been holding onto that are creating discordant vibrations around you. They are sucking away your vital energy and draining your vibrant spirit.

If you seek renewal you must pass through this narrow place. I promise that if you will summon the courage to purge your life of all that is no longer useful, you will find yourself liberated, light and free. You will be able to hear your muse's every whisper; you will see colors, hear music, and enjoy the warmth of light rediscovered, warming your soul, like sun, like warm oil on your skin.

You must purge your house of clutter, you must divest yourself of all the creepy little elementals that are hitchhiking on your aura. The free ride is over.

Judy's very heart-filled message from *heartlessness* contains a key sentence: "If you seek renewal you must pass through this narrow place." In the first five books of the Hebrew Bible, the most often repeated sentence is "I am *Adonai*, your God, who brought you out of the land of Egypt." In Hebrew, Egypt is *mitzraim*—"the narrow place." Rabbinical scholars suggest that this sentence is repeated so often as a reminder of the need for liberation from the narrow places of our thoughts, our hearts, our souls.

Much like passing painfully through the narrow birth canal, that we might live and grow, the path of spiritual alchemy calls for us to pass through "this narrow place" of our habitual self-definitions. As spiritual alchemists, we must (as *heartlessness* wisely said) "summon the courage" to divest ourselves of "all that is no longer useful."

MY OPPOSITE ISN'T YOUR OPPOSITE

The concept of opposites is both complex and subtle. The group energy in a workshop often leads to people's coming up with common symbols ("your anger was a fireplace? so was mine!"). This same energy often leads to common "dominant" traits as well: peaceful, loving, thoughtful.

Yet the opposite of "peaceful" might be *warlike* for one person but *uncentered* for another—or perhaps *angry*, *enraged*, *distracted*, or *anxious* for a third person. The opposite of "loving" can be *unloving*, *hateful*, *indifferent*, *cold*, *fearful*, or *cruel*. Rarely do any two people with the same dominant quality choose the same "opposite."

Each of us chooses the appropriate opposite voice to get the message we need. But what kinds of messages—or revelations—are they?

UNDERSTANDING THE "OPPOSITE"

Once you start writing in the opposite voice, you may discover that it is merely a part of your nature that you haven't been acknowledging. You might have chosen not to exercise it because you don't like it, or you might not have known it was part of you because you were so busy thinking of yourself as "not like that." The second most common discovery is that the opposite word not only isn't opposite—it's not the right word at all. Just as Judy's "heartlessness" wasn't heartless, Virginia's "Hard" was simply common-sensical and well-organized.

But sometimes the opposite quality is the one you need to cultivate, while the quality you think is dominant is the one you wish to believe in. In this case, you may need the opposite voice—a truer, deeper voice—to guide you in a more meaningful direction.

Remember, whatever their religion, alchemists tended to reject the simplistic notion that opposites were separate and unrelated. Recall the quotation in the introductory chapter from one of the most ancient of Jewish mystical writings, the *Sefer Yetzirah*: "God has also set one thing opposite the other; the Good opposite the Evil, and the Evil opposite the Good; Good from Good, and Evil from Good; the Good defines the Evil, and the Evil defines the Good." Likewise in *Kohelet* (Ecclesiastes), a book that some believe was written by Solomon nearly 3,000 years ago, we find "also this opposite the other did God create" (7:14).

Gnostics of all religions know that we cannot define or understand anything without being aware of its opposite. If not for the dark, we could not know light. Without the existence of evil, how would we understand the nature of good? If all that is created is infused with the divine spirit, then so must evil be—however we detest its manifestation. Gnostics, alchemists, and religious mystics (some of whom were all three) thus paid great attention to the transformative power of opposites, as should we.

"Allow me to be you"

Kathleen has always wanted to write. But with work and family obligations, she never has the time. She sees herself as having *courage*—and chooses *acceptance* as its opposite. For Kathleen, being *courageous* implies doing things and changing things, not merely *accepting* them as they are. But the voice of *acceptance* has something much different from "accepting" to tell her:

> You need to be more gentle with yourself. Don't beat yourself up because you can't sit down and take the time to write. Your fears are not the source of your aversion. You're a powerful person, and in the past the power had turned back on itself due to misuse. Sit with feeling powerful, but with love—gentle, focused power that wells up from deep inside of you. It is the balancing of this power that will allow you and me to walk hand in hand together into wholeness.

> My gentle friend, we are always the same to each other, *yin* to your *yang*, my lasting touch, your nurturing spirit are one and the same. Allow me to be you, and you me. You have the power to succeed and balance all that you do. The gift of your writing will be an outpouring of balanced spiritual power that will heal you and others. The magic is in the expression of who you are. All the parts of you, past, present, and future. Allow me to be with you; take **your** time, take **our** time. We are, you are, I AM.

The voice of *acceptance* does more than merely guide Kathleen along a gentle path. It also allows her to understand *courage* in a very new light. Her most courageous act, right now, is to follow the accepting voice back into authentic personal power.

OPPOSITES ATTRACT?

"Go ahead and smoke," Joanne begins reading, but first she has to wait for our laughter to subside. Only moments earlier, she had told us that she finally quit smoking.

Sometimes the opposite voice so powerfully names our addictions, our shadow sides, that all we can do is laugh. This voice so boldly names our unhealthy urges that we can no longer rationalize them as acceptable. In these situations, the opposite voice takes on such a negative life of its own that we can't ignore it anymore. It forces us to face ourselves and, as the saying goes, fish or cut bait. This kind of opposite voice is so clearly opposed to our welfare that it actually helps us to end its hold on us.

> Go ahead and smoke. So what if you get lung cancer and have a horrible sickness and death just as you're about to live your life. Go ahead and smoke...so what if you stink to others or your teeth are stained and your fingers smell.

> Go ahead and take that drag. Fill your lungs. Meditative breathing takes too long and it's not the same, and weight gain you don't need. Go ahead. Light one up.

So what if it wrinkles your skin and gives you that Sister Josepha hook on the right side of your bottom lip. Remember? Third grade, first seat, right row? She stood right in front of you, her perfect fingertips tapping on your desk as she looked out to the class to teach? You could smell the starch on the collar of her habit. You could see the pores on the skin and knew it was amazing that she had no wrinkles because she was so old. She just had the right hook deep in her skin on the right side of the bottom of her lip. The Sister Josepha hook that you vowed right then you'd never have.

Go ahead, smoke the damned cigarette. Take a deep inhale. Feel the packed tube in your fingers. Add a cup of coffee. Throw in a rainy day with you on the couch. A lit candle. Cigarette as friend.

Make new friends? Find things to do with your hands?

Make new friends? Find the love of your life while you still have life? Find a smoking husband because a nonsmoker won't have you and he's probably dull anyway? Who needs a man if you can have a butt?

Freedom. You sure talk about it enough. Be free to smoke. Don't let anyone tell you what to do. Be free to leave the dinner table and your friends to smoke alone at the bar. Be free to go out of the house in the winter or the rain to smoke your freedom. Be free. Go ahead—be one with your smoke.

"Writing lessons"

Some people learn the meaning of their opposite voice from the writing itself. Doris, in her 60s, is an elegant, soft-spoken woman who has never worked throughout her 40-year marriage. Suddenly her husband wants a divorce. He tells her he isn't seeing anybody, but she doesn't believe him; there are too many signs she can no longer ignore. They're still living in the same house—in separate bedrooms—and he promises her that the divorce can be amicable and that they will always remain friends. Although she knows that he can't bear to lose an argument, she is a good-hearted person who values friendship. His offer is appealing.

The dominant quality Doris names is *friendly*; the opposite, *unfriendly*. Despite the instruction to choose a situation of minor tension, she chooses the divorce and her inability to stop thinking about it. She is shocked by what she writes:

Forget about him. Why bother? He offers you only misery right now. He lies to you by implication, he pretends to be nice when he isn't, and you want to play FRIENDLY?

What a jerk! Don't even think about it. Just be cool, distant, and withdrawn. It'll drive him crazy. As long as you're friendly, it reinforces all the reasons he thinks you're a patsy. Now if you want to fake "friendly" for a while, go ahead.

But for him this is war, and pretending to be friends is a joke. Don't fake it after you've seen a lawyer and picked one. You need to know every way to get everything you want, and being friendly ain't one of them.

I'd cut his balls off if I had my druthers—with less testosterone, he'd be easier to handle. But then, it ain't my job. My job here is to wake you up and say, "Honey, snap out of it. Being a nice guy means finishing last. So be a realist. Take care of what you need to take care of yourself for the rest of your life—then take the money and run!"

The other participants' mouths are twitching. Doris is so ladylike that laughter might offend her.

Eyes wide, Doris muses, "This isn't the voice of 'unfriendly,' is it?"

"What voice do you think it is?" someone asks.

She looks surprised as she answers: "Common sense, I would say, wouldn't you?"

"Remember, Doris," someone else says, "that's *your* common sense speaking, not anyone else's, and you can have access to it whenever you want."

Doris sits with the concept. Then she looks up and surveys the group. "In that case," she says crisply, "do any of you know a good lawyer?"

A few weeks after that workshop, someone else got a remarkably similar message from the voice of *unkind*. Althea, who is scheduled to have a hysterectomy in two weeks, chooses the "minor" issue of deciding whether to tell her estranged husband about her cancer. *Unkind* tells her:

I'd keep my mouth shut. He'd just use anything I tell him against me, show no compassion, and look forward to getting his hands on my money. The kindness that Sue talked about works fine with other people but can't work with him, because he doesn't understand kindness for the sake of kindness. He only understands what he feels—and whatever it is that he feels, he can then immediately justify it as the *right* and *only* way to be and to behave.

There is no point in being kind to someone who doesn't know how to be kind for kindness' sake. *What you perceive of as the voice of unkindness is simply the voice of self-preservation.*

"Opposites" changing names

Every time you do this exercise, be open to the possibility that the voice isn't an opposite—or that whatever you named it isn't the right word. After you read what the voice has to say to you, rename it if necessary. That new, more appropriate name will help you better understand yourself, your situation, and your needs.

Sometimes, if you're lucky, your opposite voice will tell you who you are (or aren't). Sherene, an attractive woman in her 40s, goes into therapy to put behind her a lover who had cruelly abandoned her a year earlier. But now he is sending her a steady stream of emails, all designed to get her back. Her dominant quality is *feisty*; and its opposite, *doormat. Doormat* speaks:

> I would lap his messages up like milk, let him come back to me, hold me, caress me, and pretend that everything is OK again. It's both his pretense and mine. I would let his negativity lead the way, so that I react to his needs, take care of him, foster his spiritual growth (or 'pretend-spiritual' growth) while playing co-dependent, allowing him to avoid truth and to see himself as he is not.
>
> Throughout this time my health and sense of self would erode, as his muddy boots walk over me. I would absorb the shocks, the dirt, the scuffing—and I would absorb it in dutiful silence, *believing that such maternal passivity is the stuff of true love*. I would see myself as loving and therefore make all necessary excuses for being a doormat, and blind myself to the truth of my true uselessness and culpability.
>
> I would not be myself anymore. I would be someone I couldn't recognize. I would become invisible and would over time erode into nothing.
>
> *This is the doormat speaking, out of jealousy for the doormat that you are not.* [italics mine]

Sherene's doormat warns her not to confuse "maternal passivity" with "true love." It warns her that doormats are jealous, that she harbors a traitor-of-a-trait within her that might infiltrate and destroy her strength ("the doormat you are not") if she doesn't pay attention. It also tells her, in a punning sort of way, to show this sucker "the door"!

"The jig is up!"

Juliana's dilemma is a common one—what to do with an old friend who may not be a friend anymore. Laurie has money and time on her hands. She always seems to have problems that need hours of Juliana's time, and she gets angry if Juliana is too busy to listen. For Juliana—with a husband, a small child, and a job—these demands for her attention feel overwhelming, and Laurie's anger feels toxic. But Juliana is a good friend and a kind person, and she doesn't want to lose someone with whom she has so many years of history. Her dominant quality is *friendly*; its opposite, *unfriendly*. *Unfriendly* says:

> Tell her to bug off! Tell her that I don't have time for her, that I don't want to know her, that she had her day in court and the judgment's been handed down—and it's over, you hear me, it's over.
>
> Tell her, Go away, the jig is up. I have no time for your games, no patience for your lack of self-awareness, no tolerance for your needing to project your anger and pain and insecurities on me. I'm not the center of anyone's world but my own, and neither are you. I'm not your mother or healer or teacher or lover. I'm Juliana who stands on her own two feet and expects you to do the same. Expectation's the name of the game, and it's the only game in town. You meet my expectations or I blow you off. It's as simple as that. No more hand-holding through the problems you invent so that you'll feel important.
>
> Go grow up—and if you do, then come on back and we'll see if we have anything left in common. Maybe we used to, but we don't now, and I haven't a life to waste on pulling you through because you're not willing to pull your own weight.
>
> So godspeed but get out of my way. I'm on a roll, it's my life, and if you want to come along, then figure out how to keep pace—or go find someone else to trot along beside.

At first, Juliana is shocked by *unfriendly*'s approach. Then she realizes that *unfriendly* is helping her recognize her annoyance with people who won't "pull their own weight." Now that she's pulling her own weight at home and at work, and Laurie isn't, they don't share the same values and are no longer compatible. *Unfriendly*—who is annoyed and impatient but not really unfriendly—leaves the door open to a renewal of the friendship if the two women later "have anything in common." Juliana sighs, relieved to know she isn't really unfriendly.

Insights Without "Opposite" Language

Eleanor never even thinks of opposite qualities. She simply picks an issue (her car keeps dying for no apparent reason) and envisions a person who is the opposite of her:

> She's married indiscriminately so she doesn't have to do anything. He takes care of the car and all its problems. She calls him from Litchfield—

40 miles from home—and says she's stuck. The car's died. She has an AAA card in her wallet but she calls him.

He's watching "Golden Eye," part of a weekend marathon of guy movies he's planned to watch in her absence. He doesn't tell her to call AAA. He knows it's simpler, less painful in the long run, to call AAA himself, then drive to Litchfield in case she has to leave the car.

She goes into Dunkin' Donuts, orders a large iced coffee and takes it outside to sip under a red maple. She reads *West of Sumatra* in the late afternoon light until he comes.

Eleanor's reaction?

> I am both disdainful and envious of this woman. Disdainful because she won't take care of something simple for herself, even when she has all the tools at her fingertips. Envious that she can decide NOT to be responsible for something. I realize how much of the exhaustion I feel is from being responsible for absolutely everything for 12 years. Nobody else to do anything. (Just writing that down, I feel exhausted.)

Why *West of Sumatra*? Because that's a book that Eleanor has been wanting to read but doesn't have time for.

Eleanor's "opposite" scenario forces her to see the relationship between disdain and envy. She looks down on the woman because she envies her. She now knows, no matter what she tells herself, that she really wants to be in this woman's financial position: to have the luxury of choosing, even if she wouldn't make the same choices; to have the luxury of reading; to have the monkey of self-support off her back.

Getting a Glimmer

While preparing to give the very first workshop, I am staying with my parents in Oakland. My then 81-year-old mother, Gloria, is so excited for me that I ask her to join us.

"Oh, dear, I'd love to come, but I'd probably just get in the way." Since she's delighted by the invitation, it doesn't take me long to convince her. But a memorial service is to be held later that weekend for a close friend. Being the good Polish Jewish mother that she is, Gloria is up nearly half the night cooking for the after-service gathering at the home of his widow. She comes to the workshop in typical Gloria fashion: exhausted but determined—and still excited.

After the introductory comments, I ask the participants to tell each other why they've come. My mother speaks last, almost hesitantly: "I come from a different world from you young women. Oh, I realize you're not young, like children, but you're so much younger than I am, and you see things so differently. I grew up in another world, in a different country, at a different time. We didn't speak about our feelings. We didn't even think too much about them for ourselves. So I'm not even sure what I want from a workshop like this. I simply wanted to come. I hope I'm not a burden, being so tired and so slow."

Everyone praises her thoughtfulness, makes her welcome. From time to time, I see her doze off. But when we come to the opposite voice exercise, she seems more alert. After the rest of us discuss our experiences, we turn to her.

"Well, it's difficult for me to talk about certain things, as you know. What's been bothering me lately—oh, it's been bothering me for years—is something my husband does. Don't misunderstand me, he's a wonderful man and we love each other, but sometimes he uses language that he knows he shouldn't use and he knows I don't like. And after all these years, I still can't break him of the habit.

"I didn't get the beautiful writing that you got, and I think I slept through the part about the opposite words, but I got a glimmer of something I can do. And maybe it will work. Maybe if I say something similar back to him, it might shock him into stopping." A mischievous glint comes into her eyes.

I can't help raising my eyebrows. This, from my mother, who blushes if she says "darn"?

Over the next few weeks, I ask her if she's tried her new scheme. "Not yet, dear, but I will, I promise. I'm getting ready." She sounds pleased with herself. Eventually, she tells me what happens:

"We were sitting at the kitchen table, and your father got angry about something, oh, I forget what it was—maybe politics. Anyway, he began talking the way I don't like—

"'The damn bastards!' Things like that?"

"That's right, dear, that kind of language. So I sat up as tall as I could, and said very loudly, 'Oh, SHIT!!'

"He looked shocked. Then he said, 'Gloria, do you realize how *foul* you sound when you talk like that?' So I told him, 'Do you realize how foul *you* sound when you say "damn bastards"? If you don't want me to talk that way, then you'd better stop talking that way!'"

"Oh, Mother, that's brilliant!" I gasp between laughs. "Has it worked?"

"Not really." She giggles. "But *I* feel much better." ⚓

CHAPTER
6

Letting Go of Self:
Seeing Through New Eyes

As you move further along the path of spiritual alchemy, you discover that you can never see exactly where it leads. At this particular bend in the road, you are about to begin seeing through new eyes. Before you can improve your vision, however, you need to make sure that your energies are sufficiently balanced. Only then will you have the strength to see yourself clearly through new eyes, and to revisit the world in which you live from yet another perspective.

Just as one of the goals of the ancient alchemist was to transmute the *prima materia* into something rarefied and precious, another was to shift his or her inner vision to a different plane. This is what you are about to do.

BALANCING YOUR ENERGIES

The beginning of Exercise 6 involves balancing your energies—specifically, your chakra energy points—so that you are in physical and spiritual alignment. If you're not familiar with the word *chakra*, it comes from the Sanskrit word for "wheel," and refers to major energy centers within the body, beginning at the base of the spine and going up to the crown of the head. The unusual way in which you will be balancing your energies is a method that comes from the American seer Edgar Cayce. While the Jewish tradition has equally powerful ways of balancing and raising energy—and creating soul connection—using them calls for more knowledge of Hebrew and the teachings of various schools of *kabbalah* than this book can cover. Therefore, because Cayce and his work are more widely known, I turn to his remarkable knowledge and wisdom.

In traditional teachings, there are seven chakras: (1) at the base of the spine, (2) just below the navel, (3) at the solar plexus, (4) in the center of the chest, (5) at the base of the throat, (6) between the eyebrows (often called "the third eye"), and (7) at the crown of the head. These chakras are also associated with glandular functions. Most people associate the first chakra with the base of the spine, for example, and the second chakra with the gonads (sexual organs).

But Cayce's readings associate the first chakra with the gonads and the second with "the lyden"—which turns out to be the "cells of Leydig" (cells that "sit" on the ovaries in women and on the testes in men, and that produce, among other hormones, testosterone). According to Cayce, the "seat of the soul" is in the second chakra; it is the place where the soul enters the body.

In yet another important way, Cayce's understanding of the chakras and their functions differs from the common understanding. Cayce said that raising one's energy is like priming a pump: the energy has to go *higher* than the outflow point, so that it can naturally flow out or down. Thus the energy flow that starts from the first and second chakras continues to the third, which is associated with the adrenal glands; to the fourth, associated with the thymus gland; and to the fifth, associated with the thyroid gland. But when it comes to the sixth and seventh chakras, Cayce's "priming the pump" principle comes into play.

According to Cayce's readings, the sixth chakra is not, as commonly assumed, at the third eye but at the crown of the head (associated with the pineal gland). From there, the energy can naturally flow down to the third eye, the seventh chakra (associated with the pituitary gland). In other words, instead of moving in a straight line from the base of the spine to the crown of the head, the energy goes "straight" as far as the throat chakra; then it zooms up to the crown of the head, from where it "falls" or flows into the third eye.

After over a decade of work with this method, my understanding is that while we receive universal energy through the crown chakra, we connect individually to our individual soul through the third eye. We are therefore closer to the divine—to our soul—not at the crown chakra but at the third eye. This "soul-connecting" factor is the reason that you will be starting the rearranging and listening exercises with Cayce's technique for energy balancing. (Although you may have a technique of your own that works well for you, I urge you to try Cayce's for the exercises that follow.)

EXERCISE 6

Seeing Through New Eyes

For this exercise, you will be opening and closing your eyes several times: closing your eyes to follow the visualization instructions, opening them to write down what you saw, then closing them to visualize some more. Simply follow the directions on track #2 of the CD.

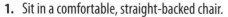

Seeing Through New Eyes

1. Sit in a comfortable, straight-backed chair.

 15 to 25 minutes

2. Start track #2 of the *Guided Visualizations* CD.

3. Close your eyes and sit with your hands clasped or palms touching in your lap.

4. Follow the directions.

When you have finished the exercise, turn the page.

WHY A MARTIAN?

While most people really enjoy the "Martian" exercise, some question its value: "It was great fun, but what does it have to do with me and my soul? How can this exercise improve my spiritual listening skills? What does it have to do with spiritual alchemy?"

For the best of all possible answers, I'll let someone's Martian do the talking. She/he/it is a savvy observer with a lot to say:

> When humans sit in silence, often for minutes or hours, they seem to become one with their chair. Yet their minds are not in the chair, because their consciousness is far away. They have two directions they can take. One is to go into a small space within, from which they enter an inner portal leading to the deepest recesses of their hearts and minds. The other is to exit their private selves and head out the double doors into the wide world and blend their consciousness with that of nature.
>
> Whether they hide in the self or disappear into a tree, only their body stays in the chair. But neither their body nor the chair matters. The humans can melt into the universe from inside or outside.
>
> *What is important is that they leave the self. As long as they are inside the self and identified with it, they cannot do good work.*

In other words, none of us can go straight from creating our inner laboratory to working with it—because being "inside the self and identified with it" keeps us from doing "good work."

That's why we have to first work with the opposite voice and the Martian voice. Until we have practiced the skills of *leaving ourselves* as we understand ourselves, we aren't ready to go to our laboratory to listen to the voice of our own soul. Before we can work in that room, we need to understand ourselves in a larger context, a wider field, a world in which our self-constructed "self" is insignificant.

One of the crucial aspects of a Martian is that we see it as alien. But a Martian is alien in our minds only because we expect it to be. We make a Martian alien before we ever meet one. We often do the same thing with other human beings: someone who eats bees, someone who has committed assault and battery, even someone who yells a lot when we tend to keep our feelings to ourselves (or vice versa)—all of these humans we tend to see as alien to our personal experience of what it means to be human. "They" are different. "They" are, in particular ways, "opposites" of us.

But a major part of coming to know ourselves is recognizing that all human beings share the potential to commit harm or do good, to eat foods we can't imagine eating, to experience different ways of expressing feelings. Central to the practice of spiritual alchemy is the no-holds-barred self-awareness that we contain all opposites. So before you can begin working in your room, you have to experience being the "alien" and, I hope, recognizing it as yourself.

Likewise, in doing the opposite voice exercise, I hope you realized that all voices are potentially yours, that there is no emotion that you can't feel or attitude you can't take *if you want to or allow yourself to*. Similarly, in the Martian exercise, you learn to integrate what you had placed outside of yourself. By doing so, you add the "alien" voice to your repertoire of voices, to the fuller truths you are learning about yourself and who you really are.

As you read the following Martian reports, you'll notice that the "pre-report" images are not three, but five. That's because I usually ask workshop participants to look to the right of the central image—and then to the right of that. I do the same for the left. So instead of working with three images, they work with five. Exercise 6A, an optional exercise at the end of this chapter, gives you the chance to try working with five—two on the right and two on the left. But whether you work with five images or three, the Martian will still have much insight for you.

The more often you do the Martian exercise, the more you work with symbols. Although you consciously chose the central image for this exercise, you then allowed your unconscious self to replace it with a symbol. The other images—to the right and the left—are likewise symbols. Among the many things that Carl Jung had to say about symbols, he made the following observation:

> There never was a genius who sat down with his pen or brush and said: "Now I am going to invent a symbol." No one can take a more or less rational thought, reached as a logical conclusion or deliberately chosen, and then disguise it as a "symbolic" phantasmagoria. No matter how fantastic the trappings may look, it would still be a *sign* hinting at a conscious thought, and not a symbol. A sign is always less than the thing it points to, and a symbol is always more than we can understand at first sight. Therefore we never stop at the sign but go on to the goal it indicates; but we remain with the symbol because it promises more than it reveals.

Writing from the Martian point of view helps you "remain with the symbol" longer and more deeply.

Martian imagery, martian insights

Martian voices come in many forms, from the humorous to the technical (some Martians use strange scientific terms) and from the pompous (some Martians, like humans, are quite full of themselves) to the humble. While their reports don't necessarily reveal deep truths about their individual authors, they almost always contain deep truths about humanity.

Joanne Peck's Martian writes:

> I have found that these humans fill themselves with the strangest things...old wounds that have been allowed to fester and grow, old pain allowed to anchor in their minds and souls until the roots crowd out any new growth.
>
> They save memories....bad ones that should have been thrown out like half-full glasses of stale beer and cigarette butts the morning after a party but are allowed to stay with them, permeating their being with the stench of decay. They carry around all of their good memories, exposing them to the light and air, and letting them fade and tarnish, instead of keeping them put away where they are safe, to be taken out, still bright and shiny, when they are needed.
>
> And the voices....mostly echoes from the past that should have long since been silenced. Mothers, fathers, taunting children, half-forgotten lovers, crying babies, spouses, friends, and even strangers—all clamoring for attention.
>
> They are full of hopes and dreams, fear and doubt, love, hate, expectations, and regrets. Why can't they learn to throw out the trash, store the treasures, and empty themselves to make room for the new and wondrous?

Joanne's Martian offers us a wake-up call, reminding us to "store" and treasure only what we value, and to "empty" ourselves so that we have room for the "new and wondrous."

IN-DEPTH MARTIAN REPORTS

Yet sometimes a Martian report reveals deep truths about its author, answering questions that he or she never thought to ask. Sandra, a troubled young woman, tells everyone at a conference for writers that she can't write. When we come to the Martian exercise, she sees symbols she doesn't understand and insists that she can't see any relationship between them. I suggest that if she doesn't understand the relationship, her Martian should be an honest reporter and say exactly that.

Here is what her Martian reports:

> From my visit to earth, I understand nothing about this strange relationship.
> I can't report on relationships because I can see none.
> On the dank dark earth, nothing was connected, nothing was in harmony.

All is disconnected like triumphant woodsticks all in a straight line, like little soldiers, waiting to take their orders and march on to the execution.

There's blood all around, dripping in sheets, thick and globby, covering everything in its path. And beneath its heavy flow lie creatures of all kinds, and I could hear their cries of sorrow and helplessness.

No one was there to offer a hand, to bring them out and lead them to salvation, as they frantically waited for a divinity that would never appear.

I saw no connections, perhaps I am blind. There's much I cannot see and much that I miss.

Your expectations scare me, I don't know if I'll be right or wrong. In my anxiety to please and get your approval, that will gave me a reason of why I should exist, I fumble, tense up, and go blind. I can see nothing, my being is taken over by the dark smoky fog that has become my cell.

I come back and get what I deserve, your anger and disgust at my stupidity and incompetence.

And so it is.

Sandra finishes reading and breaks into sobs. By reading aloud what she thought was "garbage," she suddenly sees the poisonous negativities—from parents, teachers, and others—that she has ingested over her lifetime and made her own.

Other participants offer her similar experiences of having trouble visualizing, of feeling unequal to the work. They speak of their fears, their inadequacies, their childhood issues, their familiarity with her despair. Sandra's eyes grow huge. "Then you *do* understand," she breathes. Everyone nods. She lets out a long sigh, and her voice grows incredulous. "All of you who wrote so beautifully, you've gone through this, too?"

She has heard her Martian speak—and she is no longer alone. She now has the insights to begin walking the long healing road to releasing the negatives. Whether she takes that road is her decision. Her Martian's job was to point the way.

MARTIAN "THERAPY"

Some people need the Martian voice—a voice not their own—to understand their current predicaments. For example, a self-supporting woman with money troubles sees a dollar sign ($) as her central symbol. That she should see it is no surprise—but what her Martian lets her know about it is:

I see [it observes] the horizontal wavy lines of the sign as the human pedestrial pull, and I see the vertical lines as the pull of the Universal longing to connect with the Divine. To the left, now traveling on the wavy line,

spirit—for all spirit connects to the source. A rabbit may outrun a tiger, the tiger might starve. A tiger might eat a rabbit and when the tiger dies, grasses might grow from the tiger that some other rabbit might eat.

You are the rabbit, the tiger, the fire and the halo. You are the timid, the wild, the sweet and the terrible—we all are. Polarities.

MARTIAN SURPRISES

Some Martians, like humans, are tricksters, full of illuminating surprises. Here is what happens to Helga Kelter Abramson, sitting dumbfounded in her chair, trying to figure out why her Martian report turned out so differently. She tells us she doesn't know how it happened. Her husband is the central image, and he becomes a diamond. But what pours out of her, instead of a Martian report, is "Happy Anniversary to the Diamond." Read it aloud, as she did in the workshop, so that you too may fall under the spell of its rhythm. It contains not only the opposites but also the essence of spiritual alchemy:

> I thought you ran with the wolves
> > But you did not.
> I wanted you to run with the wolves.
> > But you did not.
> I thought you would take over
> > But you did not.
> I wanted you to take over
> > But you did not.
> I thought you would lead the change
> > But you did not.
> I wanted you to lead the change
> > But you did not.
> I thought you knew what to do
> > But you did not.
> I wanted you to know what to do
> > But you did not.
> I thought you knew everything
> > But you did not.
> I wanted you to know everything
> > But you did not.
> I thought you would protect me from pain
> > But you did not.

I wanted you to protect me from pain
    But you did not.
I thought you would be my playmate
    But you are not.
I wanted you to be my playmate
    But you are not.
I thought you would help me
    And you did.
I thought I could not run with the wolves
    But I can.
I wanted you to take over and you did not
    And I can.
I thought you would lead and you did not
    And I learned I can.
I wanted you to know and you do not
    But I know.
I thought you know everything and you do not
    I will tell you.
I wanted you to protect me from pain and you did not
    I choose my own pain.
I thought you would play with me and you did not
    I invent my own games now.
Through you I have become more whole.
    I LOVE YOU

Be sure to treasure your Martian, who represents a key to your membership in humanity. Your Martian reminds you that the alien is familiar, that the alien is a wonderful teacher, and that you have met the alien—and it is you.

Having allowed your Martian to write its report, you are ready to return to your room. You may, of course, choose to first do the optional Martian exercise that follows (6A)—using five images instead of three. Either way, after you finish or skip Exercise 6A, I suggest—with no punishment intended—that you turn to the next chapter and *go to your room*! ⚓

(OPTIONAL) **EXERCISE 6A**

Seeing Farther Through New Eyes

For this exercise, you will be repeating all the steps of the previous Martian exercise. The only difference is that you will be working with *five* images.

This time, after you look to the right of the central image to see what is there, then look again to the right of that image, to see what is on the *far* right. Then do the same for the left side.

What the Martian will have to say may be more complex, depending on the Martian....

Although this exercise is optional, it will help you to continue letting go of self-focus. I strongly recommend it if you are still struggling with the practice of holding the tension between opposites or with the issue of recognizing the "alien" within yourself.

If you choose to do this exercise, follow the instructions at the beginning of this chapter—but turn instead to track #4 on the CD.

CHAPTER
7

Rearranging and Asking

The time has come for you to return to your room, to convert it into the laboratory it is meant to be and to begin learning how to use it. This chapter contains three very short exercises. You only need to do two at this time. The third you can do either now or later.

Plan to do the first two at one sitting—one right after the other. Therefore, give yourself at least 20 minutes, and up to 35, for these two exercises and the page of reading between them. You won't be disappointed!

EXERCISE 7
Rearranging

EXERCISE 7

Rearranging

1. Sit in a comfortable, straight-backed chair.

2. Start track #6 of the *Guided Visualizations* CD.

3. Close your eyes and follow the directions.

When you have finished the exercise, turn the page.

 3 to 10 minutes

Diane, a young divorced mother of three, has a large trampoline in her room, representing *never bored*. But as she looks at it, she realizes that she's never bored because she's "always bouncing up and down, up and down, never getting a chance to rest." She smiles when describing her only room change:

"I unsprung the trampoline. I made it more like a hammock that I could rest and relax in."

"You took out the tension!" someone calls out, and we start laughing. Diane looks puzzled, because the meaning of her room change was unconscious.

"You didn't just take the tension out of the trampoline," we explain. "You also took it out of yourself."

REARRANGING

Rearranging your room is an act of personal power—and therefore an act of spiritual alchemy. It puts you in charge of your laboratory, rather than at the mercy of the original furnishings. Those furnishings represented old, habitual beliefs, whereas the process of rearranging allows you to become rigorously self-observant. The process therefore places you further along the path of spiritual alchemy. Alchemists are, above all, meticulous observers of process, all the while knowing that they are part of it. In other words, alchemists are observers not only of their materials but also of their essential self. In spiritual alchemy, where the self *is* the material and the material is the self, the more you attend to the process, the deeper and richer the process becomes. The more self-aware you become, the more you refine your "material" and the greater your ongoing transformation becomes.

Reconfiguring your room, therefore, offers you more than a second chance at creative interior decorating. It also gives you another chance to reconsider your beliefs about yourself. As Carl Jung observed, "Whatever else the unconscious may be, it is a natural phenomenon that produces symbols, and these symbols prove to be meaningful." By patterning your room, writing in the opposite voice, and learning to write as a Martian, you may have discovered qualities or beliefs that you left off your original list. You may also have realized that some of those you listed are inaccurate, judgmental, or unkind. Even more important, you may now see that some of the qualities you turned into huge furniture may not loom so large in your life, whereas some of those you made small or hid in a corner are actually more central to the core of your being.

No changes

Some people, though very few, do no rearranging. They love their rooms from the start and change nothing or almost nothing. Some spend their "rearranging" time enjoying the room, perhaps moving cushions on the couch the way dogs move in circles at night before choosing a sleeping position. Others settle in happily, as if sinking gently into a feather bed. For these people, creating their room is simply like coming home.

Marsha has only seven items in her room. She adores them all:

> On the bed there is an open book, as if I was interrupted in my reading. The open book represents my *gifts as a story teller*, and the gift is resting on the bed. The bed is the focus of the entire room…. It's soft, sumptuous, downy, covered in rich blankets and fluffy pillows. The bed is substantial, and from the frame above the four posts, sheer curtains hang, giving as much or as little privacy and isolation as I desire…. The bed represents my *belief in myself as a child of the universe*, and the universe comforts and supports me in my work as a *story teller*.

If your room already gives you such clear pleasure, treasure and enjoy it.

Questioning the room

But even some of the happiest decorators still change or ask questions about their rooms. These people usually end up using their questions as springboards for learning.

Jennifer, a young psychology major, is carrying a specific emotional burden: her lack of a partner. Her rearranged room contains a dance floor with a crystal strobe light in the center. Just as she is questioning the design, bemoaning having a dance floor but no partner, she hears, "Lack is what I need to create imagination."

What Jennifer discovers is that her "partner-less" dance floor isn't empty after all. Its purpose is to give her space for creativity and imagination—a place to play and dance freely, by herself, under her own light and "in the limelight." She needs to be in the center of her own room and to stretch her imagination before she can even consider having a partner.

Cleaning the rug

Elaine, a freelance writer and mother of Jeff and Vivian, likes "the room I designed for my soul." She notices that it was full of beautiful things, "except for the hairy dog bed and the dirty carpet in the middle of it all, reflections of actual annoyances in my real home."

> They remind me that I allow a dirty house to distract me too much. I also saw the rug as a reminder of the shortcomings I feel as a mother: am I doing my best to guide my children to become positive spiritual beings? During the meditation when we fixed the room the way we wanted it, I asked: "How do I clean the rug?" The answer came: Love comes first and discipline follows. Jeff's willfulness is a positive trait—he will use it for good. Don't try to quash it too much. Vivian's self-absorption will flower into other-centeredness as she matures. Patience is needed in loving your children. Just keep cleaning the rug every day.

Elaine receives a clear message of compassionate self-discipline: *Just keep cleaning the rug every day*. To develop patience, she is to "keep cleaning" all the distractions that get in the way of loving behavior.

"They are your jewels"

In one corner of Rasma Haidri's room is a large water glass holding jewels, which represent *artistic*. She pours the shimmering jewels into her hands and lap but doesn't know what to do with them: "They are waiting to become something beautiful. I turn them in my hands, admiring their richness and color, then put them back in the jar."

Although Rasma doesn't want to change her room, she wants to know how to use it. "What do I do with all these jewels?" she asks her soul. Her answering poem informs her that "they can't stay like this, bottled up, even though the bottle is clear and pretty." She quickly learns that the jewels are for her to wear. As the following excerpt makes clear, the jewels are not just to tuck away in her pocket or hold in her lap, because "you can't wear a lap full of stones."

Even though you don't wear them yet, they know you,
they recognize you and wait. You recognize them, too,
and love their colored friendliness in your hands, in the lap
of your skirt, but look, that has been girl's play up till now....
What is stopping you? It is not the fruit on the table that gives health.
It is not the pens for writing....
None of it is what stops you.
In fact, nothing is stopping you at all.

You know this now, and hold the jewels in your hands,
waiting for the shape to form, for the jewels to enter
into something beautiful like these rugs that represent you
but were made by someone else.
Now it is your making that awaits.
They are your jewels and how you will wear them
will be of your own making.

It doesn't matter that you don't know what to do with them.
You have stopped your girl's play
and you are sitting in your deep center.
Soon your hands will know what to do
and they will take over.

Even though Rasma doesn't change her room, she uses the rearranging time to further understand it. In the process, she learns that the jewels symbolize her raw, untapped potential, both as a woman and as a writer.

When rooms need changing

But for others of us, rearranging can stir up powerful issues of integrity and choice:
- If I change my room, am I lying to myself about who I really am?
- Do I have the right to add something representing what I want to be,
  rather than how I see myself today?
- How can I throw out that "lazy" sofa if I still think I'm lazy?
- If I don't like those negative qualities but believe I have to keep them,
  how can I create a room that I *like*?

Questions like these often arise during the rearranging process. But even when major ethical issues are not involved, some people simply have trouble redecorating their rooms. Sometimes they didn't like the room from the start, don't want to return to it, and believe that they don't have the right to change anything unless they, themselves, have already changed. But just as often they simply struggle with aesthetic issues of objects and placement:

- How can I hide this hideous exercise machine? What would I replace it with if I threw it out?
- How do I get rid of the *ugliness* wall-to-wall carpeting, when it's the only rug I've got?
- Why do I have only five things in my room, when everyone else has so many? But what would I add?

These seekers often find their answers when they ask a question in their rooms—with startling results. Rona writes:

> I have to ask, Why wasn't I in my room?
>
> I wasn't ready! How could I put myself in a room of my own without knowing who I was. Things around me—only happening to me—not part of me. Now I can see, I am part of all I touch—not a passive participant in my life—my home. While I may be sitting on tentative steps, at least I placed myself there.
>
> With my bottomless bowl of yearning and hearty fork of hunger, I will be nourished on my journey. I've even grabbed my specs to see things more clearly…sometimes. I now have a home where my bed of passion has grown, and my vision of love has surmounted its frame.
>
> I can now look at my life and its contents in greater perspective—consciously positioning and tossing when needed. I will no longer hold [things] by obligation but discern what will stay with me—in my room—close to my heart, my center—all that is me. I will use my welcoming door to receive what and who I choose.
>
> This is my home—I am in it—it is me.

Notice that Rona does not distinguish between the object and the belief. Instead of saying "a bowl that stands for yearning" or "a fork representing hunger," she turns the bowl into yearning and the fork into hunger. She also has "tentative steps" and a "bed of passion."

The longer you work with your room, the more likely you are to do the same. As your furnishings become the qualities they represent, they may merge into a seamless unit that makes them more meaningful to you.

PERSISTENT TRAITS

Hilda sits at the altar in her room. She wants an answer to her question about her rebellious and willful toilet.

> Why can't I remove my toilet, which is my "needy"? I thought I could.
>
> No problem with my empty fridge, which is "unworthy at times." I just filled it up to become worthy. How good that felt.
>
> My toilet was moved to other spots by the waving of the sheer curtains, which is my music. It was missing at first, and my life is empty without it. My sheer curtains came out of my pile of clothes in the middle of the room, which is "unorganized." My toilet was moved to other spots, but it didn't fit. I even tried to hide it in the back closet but it would not stay, and finally I just allowed it to move about the room, dancing in and out of all my spots. I knew it could appear in a space without being announced, and it was OK.
>
> Yes, it is my room, and [the toilet] has a function and I must know it is a part of my room, so I will allow it to appear wherever it needs to be. It will no longer be a shame or a guilt.
>
> It can be played with and moved and rearranged and I can use it as a playful toy but **not as a crutch**. It is OK!!!
>
> Allow it to be there but let it find its place, and maybe one day it will run away to be a part of my past.

When Hilda reads her piece aloud, we laugh until our sides hurt. Our cultural norms do not usually allow us to visualize a capricious toilet that dances "in and out" of every corner, let alone a toilet that dances at all. We also gasp at the healing image of its running away "to be a part of my past."

Hilda's answer teaches two essential lessons in spiritual alchemy: First, if we are honest with ourselves, we can't remove a negative trait or behavior that still exists. Second, if we can accept that trait, free of judgment, it may leave by itself when it no longer serves us. We don't have to fight ourselves. Our job is to hold the tension, not to fight it.

Confronting the negative: to keep or not to keep?

Not surprisingly, negative traits—or, by this time, negative objects—bother most people: "I don't like having this [ugly/aging/frightened/narrow-minded/bigoted/gossipy] thing in my room," they say. "I want to get rid of it!"

Being true to yourself while removing or changing the negative is a delicate balancing act—one of the most important acts in spiritual alchemy. It calls for remaining scrupulously honest about who you believe you are, while creatively engaging with your dreams for your growing self. It is a key part of the refining aspect of alchemy: removing the dross without injuring the material. Put another way, how you deal with the negatives (which may or may not need removing) tests your commitment to the path of spiritual alchemy. Dealing with negatives in your room is your first test within your laboratory of your ability to contain the tensions—to accept and incorporate the negative rather than pretending it doesn't exist.

However, some of the negatives you have placed in your room may be other people's negatives, those you have unconsciously internalized over the years. Part of the discernment that spiritual alchemy requires is knowing whether you have outgrown them or whether they still inform your actions in this world.

At this point, the size of an object often becomes important. Ann uses a very small rug to represent all her negative traits:

> I knew I couldn't get rid of them, because they're mine and I have to acknowledge them. But I could turn them all into one object and make it very, very small. While it's a reminder of what I need to work on, it doesn't dominate the room.

Other people, like Marion, use placement:

> I don't really want to keep the bars on the front windows, but I don't want to give up what they symbolize (*strong*). Maybe I can tone it down in some way. The dark hangings (*laden by past attitudes*) on the windows are a little oppressive, too. Still, I don't want people looking in the windows from the street. Maybe I can move the windows up above eye level so they can let in light without compromising privacy.

By placing the windows differently, Marion can let go of past attitudes while maintaining her strength and her privacy. But she chooses to keep a courageous lock on her stand-offish front door, along with a cautious alarm system and a fearful peephole. Quite clear about her likes and dislikes, she says, "Let's face it. I don't want intruders, antisocial as that may sound."

But some of us are more uncertain. We're of two minds about our negative qualities and furnishings. We want to be honest with ourselves, but we don't want those unpleasant items around. We're not sure where we stand.

People who can tolerate this ambiguity will often keep the negative while admitting their discomfort with it. These brave souls face their questions head on, turning them into teachers. As one uncomfortable woman wrote:

> My inner room placed the bed (*my sexuality*) next to the *fearful* stairs (attached to the noisy door with the *brassy* doorknob, all leading to the *adventurous attic*) at the bottom right of my room.
>
> That one aspect of my room still troubles me. It seems to say that I fear my own sexuality, which I do not, as far as I know. I already feel *adventurous* in my relationship with my husband, so...?
>
> Another troubling aspect was the *agnostic* table that sat in the lower left corner, cluttered with butter (*friendly*), teapot (*gifted*), steaming cup of tea (*intuitive*). Directly above my table hung a pot of ivy (*soul-seeking*) and a gilded mirror (*truth-seeking*).
>
> I chose to keep the table, although its presence troubles me and makes my room seem incomplete—empty, rather than full. I have no chairs at this table, as this seems to denote that past company has tried to influence my place settings based on their own tastes, rather than on what I find deeply satisfying and fulfilling....
>
> I moved the bed to a more comfortable place in the room, near the *warm* fireplace, next to the rocker of *sympathy*—complete with its *dreamer* pillow.

The simple act of describing her room change gave this woman a great gift. She saw that she had unconsciously moved the bed away from fear (staircase leading to adventurous attic) to warmth and fire (warm fireplace), right next to the "sympathetic dreamer." She no longer needed to use the fearful side of her sexuality to find "high adventure." Instead, her sexuality (fire) could flow out of her natural warmth, safely "rocked" in her capacity to sympathize and dream.

BALANCING THE NEGATIVE

Another alchemical tool for handling the negative is to defuse some of its potency while balancing it with genuine positive traits—either by adding objects or enlarging them. Eileen, a teacher, does both, adding, "how revealing I found my results!"

Eileen's changes include:

- Point the shower head of generosity farther out into the room.
- Take the slip cover off of the chair of denial.
- Make that floor lamp of growing confidence as large as possible and shine it to any spot that isn't touched by the skylight of my positive nature.
- Totally dismantle the ceiling fan of hesitation.
- Remove the batteries from the smoke alarm of the inner critic and put them in the new writer's desk that is directly under the skylight; that way I control when that voice is heard.
- Get rid of that eager-to-please revolving door. Replace it with a door whose handles I control!
- Multiply those flexibility plants and put them all around the room. Then add plant stands of balance for each of them.
- Take the huge "joy laughter" sofa and make it a sectional, with pieces all over the room.

Although Eileen keeps most of her negatives, she defuses their power. She takes the batteries out of the smoke alarm and removes the slip cover from the "chair of denial." As part of balancing the negatives with positives, she points the generous shower head further out in the room, multiplies her flexibility plants, and adds plant stands for balance.

To balance the negatives with existing positives, she transforms the "huge" sofa into sectionals. Her "joy laughter" now permeates the room, so that wherever a negative exists, it has a positive counterweight. Although she "dismantles" the "ceiling fan of hesitation," she doesn't need to throw it out—because it loses much of its power by being in pieces. The same goes for the smoke alarm of the "inner critic"; without batteries, it has little "power."

Eileen then sits on a piece of her former "joy laughter sofa" and asks: "How do I hold on to this spirit when the school year returns? How do I keep the 5:15 wake-up and stacks of essays from taking over? How do I balance my work without sacrificing my pride in being a teacher?"

These are the questions of a spiritual alchemist. Instead of ignoring or wishing away the stressful demands of the world in which she lives, Eileen confronts them directly as opposing tensions in need of balancing. She understands that balance—which her life has been lacking—does not come of its own accord. It requires attention and commitment—and conscious effort.

Her answer includes clear instructions, such as "How about taking that mosaic plant stand you started to make and putting it in your new classroom as a physical reminder to keep work and personal life in better balance?"

Inner balance is Eileen's new path. It is the path of recognizing what is, refining and reshaping what she can, and allowing the rest to be itself without feeling bad about it.

FURTHER HONORING THE NEGATIVE

We all have what Jung called our "shadow," those beliefs and habits that we call "bad" or negative and wish to disown; the traits we'd like to think that others have, not us; the desires and attitudes we'd rather pretend we don't have anymore. In an exercise like this, some people find it easy to ignore their shadow sides, choosing instead to focus only on qualities they value. They often have little to rearrange, because they have "seen" themselves as wonderful and spiritual throughout.

Their lack of rearranging often reflects their fear of looking deeply into themselves and finding themselves imperfect or lacking in some way. But, as we all come to this work at different stages of our emotional and spiritual development, we can only do what we are ready to do. One benefit of doing these exercises with other people, rather than alone, is that watching others make huge emotional strides often gives the more cautious among us the courage to take some risks of their own.

THE IMPORTANCE OF HOPE

Because this is a rearranging exercise, many people focus on hope: By keeping only those qualities with which they *choose* to identify, they hope to minimize or exorcise the negative. These are generally people who have identified too long with their shadow side or with a negative self-image. (Whether that image was self-imposed or drummed into them by others doesn't matter.) When these people choose to delete the negative furnishings, they are not ignoring or denying their shadow. Instead, they are reframing their self-image by focusing on the positive. They focus on their newly discovered strengths and on their recognition that the negatives from the original room design have nothing to do with them at all.

But a very small group of people consciously decide to keep the negative traits central. They do so for reasons that often have to do with acknowledging the power and function of the shadow in their lives. For them, keeping their negative traits central stands for being true to themselves.

THE CONNIVING SURVIVOR

Charmaine is a French woman "of a certain age." When very young, she had married a 40-year-old man from another country. Both handsome and ambitious, he seemed the perfect ticket out of her parents' repressive—and poor—French Catholic home. She soon has money, status, and passion. But within a few years, her husband informs her that he has now reached the age when he can be "done" with sex. Although she stays faithful as long as she can, her strong sexuality eventually leads her to short-term affairs. Because having affairs is socially acceptable in Paris, she feels no shame. Ironically, she doesn't really enjoy them.

Over the years, Charmaine gives up her affairs. She is 60 and has come to love her husband in a sisterly way. It seems a fair trade for the expensive creature comforts and social status. Then her husband makes a rash business decision and completely jeopardizes their finances. With bankruptcy imminent, they throw themselves on the mercy of his wealthy but nasty cousin in suburban Connecticut.

Although they lose everything, the cousin lets them live in his small guest house. Charmaine helplessly watches her husband's self-confidence evaporate as the cousin turns him into a servant. Soon, to her total surprise, she falls in love with a younger neighbor and begins the most passionate sexual relationship of her life. They have been meeting secretly for five years. When she speaks of "Bill," she glows.

Charmaine's Room

When she first names and arranges her room, it contains only twelve items:

- heavy oak table (I have lived before, I live now, I will live again, I will learn)
- a very dark cupboard (sexual, sensual, sexually amoral yet faithful) [She can't be sexually unfaithful, she says, to a husband who doesn't want sex]
- delicate bone china (truthful yet lying)
- large sofa (loving yet devious)
- high-backed wooden chair (no longer self-deluding)
- brass buckets (sometimes bossy)
- drapes (artistic)
- light fixtures (optimistic)
- cushions (conniving)

- king-sized four-poster bed (SURVIVOR)
- deep pile carpet (nest maker)
- silverware (helper)

Doing the exercises, Charmaine realizes that she is necessary to both her husband and Bill. She recognizes that she needs them as well.

Her rearranged room has only two objects: the *survivor* bed and the *conniving* cushions. She now knows herself to be a "conniving survivor." She says these words to us with a sweet, self-knowing smile. She is proud of surviving—and if, to survive, she has to be conniving, she can accept it. What to someone else would be a negative to remove from the room is to Charmaine a negative worth honoring. While being conniving may not have been her first choice, it is still her choice, and she can live comfortably with that self-knowledge.

THE SOLITARY MAN

Mateus, a "40-something" computer genius, has a manner that appears arrogant. Some of the participants feel looked down upon. He uses complex words they don't know. His parents are European Argentineans, and he makes fun of American attitudes. We wonder why he has come, until he begins describing his room.

"My room is a cell," he says. "I am in solitary."

His cell is windowless, small, and ugly. Nothing in the room represents hope or joy. He has no positive furnishings.

We no longer think him arrogant. We see him in some terrible pain we cannot understand. As he gives no details, we will never know if the pain is personal, political, or both. But by the time we finish rearranging our rooms, he seems happy. He tells us that his room has much improved. We are eager to hear how he has transformed it.

"I took everything out," he smiles. "The cell is empty now."

A shocked silence ensues. I ask him, "How does it feel now, being empty?"

"Very good," he says. "I can live with it."

During the final exercise, he has a vision that transforms his countenance. Arrogance softens, his face lights up. But at the moment of the empty cell, all we sense is his pleasure in removing the negative furnishings. His emotional burden, however heavy, has lightened. He can "live with it."

APPLYING THE WORK

Beyond the obvious helpfulness of insight, one question remains: So what? I name myself, I arrange a room, I pattern a room, I rearrange a room, I can ask questions in it. So what? What does this have to do with my spiritual development? How is this spiritual alchemy?

The answer is application—how you will apply this work in your daily life. What you have done so far is merely the groundwork. The question now is, will you choose to become a spiritual alchemist? And, if you do, how will you go about it?

The next chapter gives you an exercise for using the room to receive questions, answers, or messages from your soul. But, to apply the insights from rearranging and having questions answered, you don't have to wait for another exercise. Right now, you can apply what you've done so far by simply *becoming in the world who you've become in your room.*

Poet and Maryland Artist-in-Residence Carol Peck shows this process in action, when she makes a clear decision in her life and connects it to changes she made in her room. Teaching poetry to elementary and middle school children on an island in the Chesapeake Bay, she is caught between the school's time preferences and her professional instincts. The school wants her to give her workshops on consecutive days, rather than her usual approach of teaching every other day, two days a week. The school's schedule would leave her almost no time to get all the children's poems typed and printed into booklets overnight, because she will be working with about 75 of them each day. Nonetheless, she is "adamant" about printing all the poems.

> If you choose half a dozen poems to read aloud the next time, the message the kids get is, "So-and-so is good at this and I am not." Every child's poem has something praiseworthy about it, and seeing their work in print and hearing what you praise about each poem spurs the kids on to dare and risk even more, to try even harder, for vivid language and metaphor. Thus they grow as writers.
>
> Unfortunately, I, and the poets I have trained, are the only ones committed to this way of working. There has been some pressure on me to change it, so other poets will not suffer by comparison, but I just cannot do that. They are stuck with my M.O. as long as I am in the program.
>
> When I mentally rearranged my room in your workshop, I threw out hesitancy and guilt!

By throwing hesitancy and guilt out of her room, Carol also threw them out of her life.

THE LIGHTER THE LOAD—THE LOWER THE COST

Kim Benson, a young married woman, has "a heavy heart and an angry state of mind." Now that she is finally living in a city she loves, her husband is applying for a veterinary residency out of state. Although she has supported his bid for a residency, she is feeling "stuck and sad."

Kim loves the process of creating the room. Hers feels "just perfect...bright and comforting." When she rearranges it, she adds a bicycle on the porch, where she can see it.

> I sit in this room and ask myself the big questions: Are we moving? Where are we moving? I'm having a hard time enjoying my lovely room because I keep looking outside wondering if I'm going to have to leave it.
>
> Then I see the bicycle waiting for me on the porch. I added the bike because in the last year I have discovered my own health and fitness. I wonder if I associate this new self too closely with my Madison lifestyle and if that's why I'm so afraid to leave. But I can take the bike anywhere. It reminds me that wellness is totally portable! The bike symbolizes my free spirit. It symbolizes adventure.
>
> I very easily created this room today. I knew what belongings I needed and how I wanted them around me. Maybe I should think about how I create a room—a space, a place—in real life. I remember how surprised we were that we settled so easily into Madison. But maybe it's not the place at all. Maybe it's us. The message I get from this is "stay" or "go"—the room goes with you. The room is really only a physical manifestation of your dreams, your beliefs and ideas, your self-concept, your happiness, your sense of peace...and you can rebuild it anywhere.

Kim then begins thinking about her recent impulse to sell their furniture and get rid of wedding gifts still in boxes and other things that don't "belong."

> But maybe it's not just about physical belongings but about emotional and spiritual belongings as well. The lighter the load—the lower the cost.
>
> That which doesn't enrich us clutters our rooms and our hearts. It makes us weary of each other and ourselves. We've got to be able to move around in our room, our place on earth. Now, I look back at the picture of my room and see that I made sure I had "room to dance." Movement is necessary. The body, the spirit, the soul, love, life. They all need movement.
>
> So again, the big question: Are we moving?
>
> I hope so.

Kim and her husband relocate to Davis, California. "California suits us," she writes. "All our family and friends responded to the news with 'of course, California is so you.' Who knew?!"

GETTING READY TO WORK

The room of yourself is now your inner laboratory. It represents the best of you, the most honest that you can be at this moment. You've moved a lot of heavy interior furniture today, and you deserve a break. So get comfortable in your room. Settle in, get to know it. Put your feet up on the couch, turn on some soothing music. Make yourself at home.

Relaxed? Good—because now it's time to put the room to work. It's time to become a practicing alchemist. It's time to start receiving messages from the voice of your own soul. ⚎

CHAPTER 8

Connecting Heart to Spirit

Y ou are now about to do the work you came to do in the first place: to listen to the voice of your own soul and to learn what it wants you to hear, see, and know.

In this exercise, you will learn how to listen without asking, how to listen in silence. How to sit in your laboratory and receive without expectation. Above all, how to receive even "nothing" and know that, when the time is right, you will always receive what you need.

Exercise 8 is different from the earlier exercises, because it includes concentrating quietly in silence for at least five minutes. During that time my voice on the CD will give you a reminder or two, to keep you focused. When the five minutes are up, the instructions will resume.

While the entire exercise won't last longer than 10 or 15 minutes, it will open and energize your chakras in an unusual way. Therefore, the extra 5 to 10 minutes are mandatory—absolutely essential—for rebalancing your energies after you have finished the exercise. Rebalancing includes listening to track #10 on the CD and having something healthy to eat, to ground you further in your body.

Be certain that you are completely rebalanced after this exercise before you drive a car or begin operating any kind of machinery.

men and women live healthier, happier lives. When the time comes to sit in her heart, Regina can bear only a minute, because her compassion instantly goes out to all who are unloved, unwanted, and uncared for. She discovers that her love has no boundaries, and she is suddenly filled with their pain. Tears roll down her cheeks.

She breaks off the exercise. "It doesn't work," she says.

Over the years she discovers her need to develop boundaries—and does. The boundaries allow her to maintain the love she has for others without becoming mired in pain for their suffering. She remains full of compassion, but now the feelings bring her joy.

FEELING THE HEART

Overall, people find sitting in the heart peaceful, soothing, warming, or healing. They are often stunned by the depth and immediacy of the experience. As Nancy Dunham said:

> Something occurred as quite a surprise to me. During the "heart chakra" exercise, in which I really took the time to center my heart, I had a vision which rose totally unexpectedly and uncalled. I saw a baby sitting in a small bubble of light, floating across the darkness. I don't know how, but I knew that baby was my mother. At that moment, the following poem was given to me:

Heart Chakra

A meditation turns
mother to child,
before pain was born.

Luminous bubble,
floating
on a field of midnight.

Inside, rising,
baby-hand reaching
toward the slippery light.

Or hungry grasp,
too soon to claim
an ancient darkness.

God yet grants
more time,
and whispers:
Recognize child and choice.

A year later Nancy writes:

"About a week after the workshop, I went to visit my mother, who was living alone in Florida at the time. My mother has always been a difficult person, and she and I had never really been very close. That poem, however, prompted me to see her in a new light.

"During my visit, I found her to be profoundly depressed; frighteningly so. We talked a lot, with an intimacy which we had never before experienced. My mother agreed to move here, to be close to me, my sister, and her grandchildren. She's been here for 10 months and, while she's still struggling with her depression, I believe her life is much improved.

"The best thing for me is that, for the first time in my life, I have a close, unguarded relationship with her. That is something I had long ago resigned myself to having to live without."

Another woman, a very forthright person, got a direct message from her heart:

> I've needed opening. You've had me closed for too long. You've meant well—it's not that you don't care for people—but you've been too preoccupied with self to be truly open.
>
> Let go of self—not just of expectations of husband, of parents, of kids—but even of self. Let go of self-absorption.
>
> Go out into the larger picture, the full image, the greater scope of things—and get off your behind and CREATE.

She tells us that she has received messages before, not realizing that they were from her soul; and that her soul has always spoken so bluntly to her, as the only way of getting her attention.

LISTENING FROM THE THIRD EYE

The "third eye," as I mentioned earlier, is the energy center at which we connect with the divine as *individuals*. That is why the exercise calls for you to go from your heart directly to your third eye.

To hear your purest soul voice, you need to begin with the heart as your base and your third eye as the focal point. By staying in the heart for at least five minutes, you build up the base, the positive "gratitude" energy, for communing with your soul. Once you have reaffirmed your love for yourself and others, the third eye will connect you with the divine. Going straight to the third eye, without the heart preparation, doesn't yield the same results. Somehow, when you move through love, you open clearer channels to the voice of your soul.

pulse, I saw the figure's face, dimly, and felt warm all over. Slowly, with three more pulses, the figure dimmed to violet, then blue, then green, and then I opened my eyes, my heart still hammering.

𝍫

From the violet pulsing of my third eye, I see and feel the web of love that connects my spirit with all who have crossed my path, who bring in transformation, healing, strength. My connections are broad and deep. They are of the heart, they are a current of light, a pulse of love.

I revel in the richness of this fabric, the texture, the color, the way it warms me in the cold, the way it shelters me from harsh weather, letting me absorb what I need from what life brings.

Now I cut with silver scissors the cords of the web that bind me to [those who have done me harm]. They can take their rightful place in the background, in the landscape of my past: only the lessons are carried forward. I sever all other connection with them.

As gratitude—gold light, thick and sweet as honey—runs through, I thank the universe for allowing me this glimpse of my big picture.

𝍫

I see a vision of the global earth, green and brown and blue encircled by swirling purple energy. Then, these words:

Walk softly on the earth.

Carry only what you need.

Everything you need is within you.

This last person writes: "I did not share any of this out loud at the workshop. I'm not sure why. But it has been a gift to share it with you now. I am contemplating writing a book about the three concepts and their practical, daily applications, and that fills me with a sense of excitement and joy."

SPEAKING IN IMAGERY

The soul voice speaks sometimes in images, sometimes in words. If we are ready for the message, we can understand it. If we are not ready, we will not be able to interpret what we have received. So if there is a discontinuity between what you know and what you hear, you may think that the soul voice is unclear or misleading, or that you have heard it wrong. If that happens, remember that all messages lose something in translation—and that the "fault," if there is one, may lie in expecting the soul voice to speak in everyday language, on a 24-hour clock, on local time.

SOUL VOICE MYSTERY AND MAGIC

At the first workshop that Rasma Haidri attends, several of us comment on the three-toned leather bag she carries, with pockets for pens, notebooks, and other things that writers love to carry. She bought it in India, she says, on a trip with her mother.

In her third-eye meditation, she sees "a reddish misty light, a tiny distant bed with a figure under a white sheet." What she writes next surprises her: a long poem about a doll's bed and her mother, about buying the purse with her mother. The poem ends like this:

> So now it is yours and for a long time it carried this smell,
> the one you recognize now in this room
> where the little bed hovers in red light.
> It is wrapped tightly in a melon-colored blanket,
> a silver sheet folded over at the head,
> and another silver, the silver of your mother's hair—
> how tightly she is cocooned, wrapped like a mummy in the bed,
> like she wrapped you as a child, *Make me a mummy*! you'd cry
> and she'd tighten the blankets on all sides and under your feet
> snuggling you in for the night.
>
> You did this later with your husband, you do it with your daughters,
> but it is not you who has now tucked her in,
> laid her down here where she is not sleeping, but waiting
> or already gone—it doesn't matter,
> this is just a bed, wrapped in coral linen, small like a doll's bed
> or far away, nearing the funeral pyre.

A hush falls as Rasma finishes reading. We ask her if she knows what it means. No, she says. Her mother is a widow in good health. "Funeral pyre," "mummy," and the Indian purse remind someone of *suttee*, the ancient Hindu practice of burning the widow along with the body of her dead husband. But Rasma's father died years ago, and her mother is not a Hindu. We are puzzled.

I later hear from Rasma that her mother died, "sudden and unexpected," four months to the day after she wrote the poem.

DISTINGUISHING THE VOICES

The pure soul voice tends to have a simplicity, both in vocabulary and sentence structure, that ordinary "conscious voice" writing does not. Not that subconscious or other voices cannot be helpful—they often are. But they sound different, because they sound too much like us.

In Exercises 7 (asking a question) and 8 (listening in silence), Rosemary Kenny received such very different answers—in such very different voices—that she was able to viscerally experience the contrast between the two:

My question was, "What is it my soul requires?"

Your soul requires space—some amount of physical space, yes, but freedom from all the activities you have been immersed in for years and years. One of the reasons your writing has become so important to you is that it is a way to move into all kinds of subjects, areas, planes from the ease of your writing chair. It is not known at this time whether this next period of quiet reflection and spiritual deepening will be temporary or permanent. That will depend greatly on what you choose. But for this time now—quiet, solitary activity will find itself your major pursuit. This change in your life will demand discipline, awareness, and firmness on your part. You will develop new habits, new skills, new assertiveness, new energy, a renewed life.

In the final exercise, Rosemary saw the following vision with her "inner eye":

A small cottage, surrounded by flowers. It almost seems to be made out of flowers, so much a part of the surrounding landscape is it. It is as though the cottage has grown out of the earth. There are pink roses climbing up one side of it. The peaked roof is blue green with overlapping wood shakes making it seem as though the cottage is capped with vegetation. Surrounding the cottage are all kinds of old-fashioned flowers—hollyhocks in crimson, white, and pink; delphinia—sky blue; snap dragons in a myriad of pastel colors, green canterbury bells. Moving away from the surrounding garden is a fringe of trees extending in a semi-circle from one side of the cottage around the back to the other side. All is vibrant with vital energy, serene, and delightful to the soul.

My question: What are you?

"I am your soul properly nourished. I am beauty and light and life. I am your sanctuary and your nourishment. Tend me well."

Rosemary then wrote her understanding of the difference between these voices:

If someone were to ask me what distinguishes the first message from the second, I would say that the first message lacks the simplicity, directness, and the forcefulness of the second response. *There is always a freshness that comes with the soul voice.* In the first passage, it is not that the communication is so far off the mark, but it has a tired, almost rehearsed quality about it; the insights are not so much insights as information. It lacks *the vigor or peaceful urgency of the soul voice* passage." [italics mine]

In her letter to me, she adds: "Natalie, as you may remember, I had told the group earlier that the only place I wanted to be was sitting in front of the balcony doors in my living room, looking out on and drinking in the green grass, trees, sun, sky, birds. I had actually begun to wonder if my strong need for doing this was in some way unhealthy. This communication from my soul brought me much relief. This is a time in my life when I am to receive and be nourished, and my sense is that this time is a spiritual preparation for who knows what."

WHAT NEXT

At this point, you have done all the exercises and made them yours. But were they hard or easy? Did you struggle with any? Did you find yourself not wanting to do one or more? Did you find yourself resisting doing the work at all?

Here is where we need to take a clear look at this struggle: the alchemist's struggle. Thousands of years of alchemical practice—and individual devotion to the practice—point to the difficulties that accompany it. The next two chapters will introduce you to the struggles of others, to the ways in which they felt they had "done it wrong" and the ways in which they found reasons for avoiding or resisting the work. Even if you were one of the few who felt no anxiety or resistance, or were not tempted to put the book down and walk away from it, these chapters have much to offer you about the depth and power of walking the path of spiritual alchemy.

The final two chapters will take you further along your path. They will show you not only how others have developed their practice but also how you can continue to develop and deepen yours. But before you turn the page, be certain to play track #10 of the CD (if you haven't already done so) to rebalance your energies. ⚡

PART THREE

THE PRACTICE

Doing It "Wrong"

While making my list of furnishings, I look up to check on the group. Everyone but one woman is scribbling away. I smile at her, as if to say "great, you're quick, you're already done." But she shakes her head, shrugs her shoulders. Something isn't going well. I gesture to the back of the room, where we sit and talk in whispers.

"What's happening, Shelley?"

"I'm finished."

"That's wonderful."

"No, it isn't. I can't make a room."

Over and over, time and again, I meet people who can't pattern, can't visualize, can't hear, can't create. They say:

"Nothing happened."

"I didn't visualize anything."

"I can't find any patterns in my list."

"I screwed up: I put the top part at the bottom."

"I must have heard you wrong, because I thought we were supposed to write in the opposite of the opposite voice."

These comments, and dozens like them, add up to the same shameful, frightening message: "I did it *wrong*!!"

All the way back to kindergarten and pre-school, the greatest fear for most of us was doing it "wrong." Instantly we became failures. We also fell prey to the taunting of the kids who got it "right," who didn't mess up, who didn't wet their pants in class or raise their hands with the wrong answers. Pleasing our teachers was no less critical than pleasing those who raised us. Except for the few of us who compensated by being wrong on purpose (daring the teacher to "do something about it"), we grew up with school-as-fear: fear of doing it wrong.

As you continue to work with these exercises, remember this: Whatever comes up for you—even if it's a blank or writer's block or Resistance with a capital R—it's authentic and it's valuable. Because the laboratory is so uniquely yours, any way that you do the exercises is right for you. There is no such thing as "the wrong way."

But no matter how much I emphasize this message, the need to please the teacher will invariably kick in. Somebody will have done an exercise "wrong"—and that person will be mortified or disheartened.

So what does "wrong" mean? That we aren't perfect? (What's new about that?) That we didn't follow directions? That we are poor listeners? Perhaps. But maybe it also means that we're highly imaginative and intuitive. Better yet, maybe it means that our intuition is guiding us to do an exercise in precisely the way that we need to do it. Maybe doing it "wrong" helps remind us that none of us are clones, that we process information differently, and that our soul voice guides us in different ways.

Sitting in the back of the room with Shelley, I suggest that free association can be daunting if she's not used to it.

"No," she says quietly, "it's not that. I don't belong here. Because I'm finished."

She shows me her list of beliefs about herself. It contains one word—"finished." Her piece of furniture for "finished" is a magic carpet, complete with steering wheel and driver's seat. Telling me her history of conforming to whatever was asked of her in school, she gives me her two new revelations: "I don't exist anymore, and I don't have to do this exercise. I'm finished."

"Finished" for her implies the end of a life, the end of her growth as a person. As she forms the word "finished," her voice trembles. Close to tears, in almost less than a whisper, she repeats, "This is so weird. This is so weird."

I ask her permission to ask my soul voice to help her understand what's going on. She nods, bending forward eagerly.

I listen, then tell her what I hear: "Shelley needs a bridge. Shelley can find her room if she has a bridge. Her magic carpet will be the bridge to help her find her room and discover who she is." As the words leave my mouth, I instantly know something else: that the magic carpet will lead her to her room—in which her furniture will be waiting. She is then to discover what each of the pieces represents. Instead of having beliefs become furniture, she needs to have the furniture before she can find her beliefs.

When I share that insight with her, joy fills her eyes. Color returns to her cheeks.

"Yes," she whispers, "I can do this."

Later she tells us that before our conversation, she had wondered if the magic carpet was Wonder Woman's invisible plane, "and there I am with the gold lasso of Truth." But the word "finished" had kept her stuck and miserable until she heard the message about the bridge. She then flew on her well-equipped magic carpet until she saw a rectangular *kiva* with a wooden ladder access. Inside were benches on two sides, a fire pit, poles across the ceiling "for beams and structure," and smooth tawny walls. She could see light from the fire and an entrance hole, showing stars in the sky. A mask sat on one wall. Golden mysterious motes of dust danced in the air.

In her notes Shelley writes: "I am becoming the crone." During the patterning exercise, she discovers that "the room is not FIXED!" She is not "finished." The room, like her, is open to change, and "all is warm and smooth and just as it is intended to be."

When I hear from her a few years later, she is truly the crone—a strong, self-aware woman past childbearing age, a wise woman who knows her own faults and takes no garbage from anyone. She has also relocated to the Southwest.

Shelley's story beautifully epitomizes our human uniqueness. No two of us are wired exactly the same way, no two of us think alike. Certainly none of us see identical objects or visions in our imaginations or our dreams.

For most people, profound self-understanding comes from the act of creating the room of the self. But for Shelley, that deep understanding needed to come from discovering the room first. She had to discover herself anew, because the old, family-instilled messages telling her she was "finished" had prevented her from creating a room piece by piece. Shelley needed to use the tools at hand—her own tools—to discover and understand, rather than to create and understand.

Helping Shelley find her room taught me that, in constructing our inner laboratory, there are as many "right" ways as there are people. She taught me that the exercise is a tool that we make our own, in our own way, and that each person who "does it wrong" expands for the rest of us our understanding of how the process works. To paraphrase an old saying, one person's "wrong" is another person's "right." (In later workshops, I found that if I did not have the necessary inspiration to help someone who needed to do the work differently, one of the participants would have the answer. Or a question of mine or someone else's would spark an idea for the person who was stuck. This is yet another value of doing the work or sharing the results with others.)

For all of the exercises in this book, "doing it wrong" usually takes one of four forms. The three most common are *forgetting, misunderstanding,* and *feeling inadequate.* The fourth, *resisting*, is not only more dramatic but also surprisingly fruitful. Even if resistant participants cannot see the source of their resistance, the rest of us can—and we invariably learn a lot from it.

FORGETTING

Forgetting fascinates me, because I used to remember everything, from directions to buildings in cities I'd never revisited to names of camp counselors from 15 years earlier. I could quote conversations by heart. But one afternoon in my late twenties, I began "forgetting" to make certain phone calls or to meet certain people for lunch. What was going on?

Forgetting, although sometimes physiological in origin (aging, brain damage, attention deficit disorder), makes itself useful in curious ways. For people whose real desires have gone underground, forgetting allows them to do what they want without breaking the rules that they consciously live by. That's the kind of forgetting I did. Although finally ready to live by my own desires, I still couldn't let go of my image of myself as "not hurting anybody's feelings" (that is, never saying "no" to anyone). Not surprisingly, I am the daughter of a well-behaved, determinedly good "old country" mother who could always one-up me in forgetting. She would simply follow her feelings, regardless of consequence, then say quite sincerely, "Oh, I'm sorry, dear, I just didn't think!"

Both not thinking and not remembering serve the same unconscious purpose.

But for spiritual alchemists working in our inner laboratories, the act of forgetting serves a positive and important function. Forgetting tricks those of us who are "forgetful" into making discoveries that our conscious minds are unable to make. Forgetting puts us on the right track and leads to insight. It is the psyche's gift to itself. It is one of the many unconscious tools of spiritual alchemy.

Forgetting Furniture

Sophia is an immensely prolific, creative teacher and writer. With a mind like a sharp razor, she misses nothing, down to the most subtle psychological cues. So when Sophia "forgets" something, she immediately pays attention. Her act of forgetting took place while she was designing her room.

> Despite going over the list of furnishings three or four times to make sure I'd forgotten nothing, I still forgot the mirror which represented *not being perceived accurately*. When I finally get the mirror in the room, it reflects both self-sufficiency (*a large fountain*) and heaviness (*a marble statue*). Forming a triangle with the mirror (and visible from certain angles in the mirror) is the computer representing the *gap between what I do and what is important for me to do*. The third point in the triangle is humor (*a large, whimsical fork-art carving*).
>
> Between the mirror and the humor is a huge threadbare Cabistan carpet representing *too old to be desirable*; it is surrounded by large, brightly colored pillows representing *kindness*. It struck me that to get at both the humor and the important work AND to get an accurate reflection of my reality, I should probably use a little kindness to mitigate some of the judgments I make about myself.
>
> And perhaps the *heaviness* and *self-sufficiency* need to go a bit off to the side so that they don't take up all the space in the mirror. If that's all I can see in the mirror, I may miss what's important and what's fun!

Although other aspects of the exercise interested her, Sophia felt that the mirror and what it reflected seemed critical. After reading her patterning piece aloud, she asked, "If I've forgotten the mirror repeatedly, is it *I* who am not perceiving myself accurately, rather than others?"

Several people immediately agreed. One asked Sophia why she had something in her room that represented other people's perceptions of her. Since the room was to contain only her own images of herself, perhaps the mirror stood for other people's reflecting a self-image that she wasn't yet recognizing.

But, the speaker continued, could the mirror also represent deep feelings she had about being inaccurately perceived?

"Definitely the second," said Sophia. "Very deep feelings—they're called fear."

Sophia later shares with me a series of relationships, going back to early family history, of psychologically disturbed people who perceived her creative, innocent, and ethical behavior through distorted lenses and punished her for whatever they thought they saw. No wonder she feared putting the mirror in the room—and no wonder she "forgot" to do so. Understanding her "forgetting" eventually allowed her to put her fears in perspective and put her mirror in her room.

MISUNDERSTANDING

"Misunderstanding" covers the complex, intricate, and highly creative ways in which people mis-hear, misinterpret, or misunderstand the instructions for an exercise. At first, I blamed myself ("I must not have been clear enough"). Yet, without fail, everybody in the room except the "mis-hearer" had followed the instructions accurately. Whenever I would apologize for having been unclear, the other participants would stop me, insisting that they had understood me and hinting that the "mis-hearer" had a problem.

I soon came to appreciate the unconscious wisdom of the misunderstanding process. Those who "misunderstood" me invariably received at least one crucial insight that couldn't have emerged had they done the exercise the "right" way. Their "misunderstanding" turned out to be yet another sign of the unconscious at work.

Being Too Literal

Miriam, an intellectual in a Ph.D. program, took my instructions literally: "Furnish your room," to her, meant *furniture*—nothing else. My next sentence, explaining that "furnish" referred to anything one could put in a room, from doorknobs to forks, went right past her.

In Miriam's case, "doing it wrong"—using an article of clothing—didn't bother her. She chose to disobey what she thought were my instructions, and that very choice led to her most valuable insight:

> I wasn't entirely faithful to your instructions. In the list of furniture, I included a pair of shoes. The shoes represented my fear. When I got to placing furniture in the room, I really did forget what the shoes were about and I left them till last. Not knowing what to do with them, I dropped them into the center of the room—right there for anyone (ME) to trip on again and again. Well, if that ain't the truth: my fear lives right in the center of my writing/living room and I let myself get tripped up by it all the time. That was a deep, deep learning.
>
> As I think about that again now—how many months later?—I realize I still have to deal with it, though a little less than before. Maybe one of the shoes is tucked under the couch a bit....

"I love solitude"

Lucy, in the "opposite voice" exercise, had chosen "I love solitude of forest" as her dominant quality, and "noise" as the opposite. Misunderstanding the instructions to write in the opposite voice, she wrote *about* the opposite voice. Although she already knew that she didn't like noise, her mis-hearing gave her a deeper appreciation of her need for solitude:

> The opposite quality—noise—needs the noise perhaps to quiet the demons that lurk in their lives. Endless chatter about nothing, loud R&B to blanket the quietness of solitude. To me solitude can be a calming and quieting form of therapy.
>
> I don't understand why "noisiness" is so preferred over solitude. The answer is revealing itself—it's coming—
>
> I try to respect a person's right to solitude, and I want the same in return.... Yet, when I'm in the presence of a very verbal and vocal person, sometimes I want to just get away for solitude. I realize the importance of communicating with one another and don't intend to shut people out, but I need my solitude.

Misinterpreting the instructions almost always leads the mis-hearer to deep self-awareness. Usually, these participants come away grateful for the insight—and for their so-called mistakes.

FEELING INADEQUATE

Doing the visualization exercise with the central symbol flanked by two images on either side is easy for Susan Davis of New York. Her primary image is her mother. To the right is a prayer book, and to the right of that, a bud vase with a red rose. To the left of her mother is a glazed porcelain vase, and to the left of that, a carved jade Buddha. A rocking chair symbolizes the mother.

But converting her personal symbols into an impersonal Martian report brings Susan up against a blank wall. While the others are writing, she comes over to where I'm sitting.

"I *can't* be a Martian," she whispers. "This is too personal."

"That's the point of the exercise, to stretch us beyond the personal."

"But not this," she insists. "It's about my mother, and it's too close, too personal. I don't know how to do what you want!"

"Well, why don't you write, from the Martian's point of view, about human beings' relationships with their mothers?"

"Ah...."

Honoring the mother is a very strange process for human beings. Because they are very close to their mothers (or at least they want to be) they have a hard time letting go of them. And the process of letting go of honoring the person, instead of the relationship, seems to be very hard. Humans seem to want their mothers to be there for them forever (no matter how old they become). That is what the rocking chair symbolizes (the mother rocking the needy child).

But mothers can't live in human form forever. They have to continue their journey as a soul on other levels of being. And so they have to separate from their children. Yes, humans can honor their mothers with gifts of prayers and roses. But ultimately the mother has to journey on alone, to leave this temporal world, to take the beautifully painted and glazed vase of her soul and to journey toward the divine, represented here as an exquisitely carved jade Buddha. The child must say to the mother: "Good-bye, Mother. God speed you on your journey."

As Susan reads her piece through tears, she has no need to explain her feelings about her mother's aging. A few weeks later she writes, "I had a wonderful time celebrating Mother's 95th birthday in Wisconsin.... A very enriching, loving experience, made all the more fulfilling because of that wisdom I received."

FEAR OF EXPOSURE AND HIDING DESPAIR

Naturally, some people who feel inadequate never speak up. Ironically, their self-protective silence denies them the help and healing they could otherwise receive. They hold their inadequacies to their chests as tightly as a poker hand. Silent for the most part, speaking tentatively if they speak at all, they give none of us a chance to help. Some come to me after everyone else leaves, eyes fighting tears or heads hung low—or send me post-workshop emails from a safe distance.

Margaretta calls a week after the workshop, asking if I can recommend a psychic to give her a reading. I remind her that she can "go to her room" and get the information for herself. But I sense that she doesn't believe me. So I encourage her to voice any thoughts or feelings about the workshop. When all of her anxieties and disappointments start tumbling out, I ask her to put them in writing:

During the exercise [of furnishing the room] I felt like a child. Someone who could not communicate, someone who had no joy, brilliance, or direction. Everything was placed there, not settled in, like it was resting on a

2-dimensional space, like it was for show and not real. Felt shallow. Felt like the words were what other people wanted me to be, but that I had no idea who I was at all.

When I added joy and hope to the room, it felt more comfortable, but I am still at odds. Nothing in my life feels right at this time. Felt like I was tolerated at the class, but not really supposed to be there. Felt a desperation for answers, but that I was not worthy enough to have them. Not having a reading exaggerated this. Like I am not a priority to anyone. Swirling through desperate spirals of questioning...self-worth, love of self, stance, and life value. Rocks of shortcomings battering me as I spin without a direction. Selfishness, unwillingness, fear, helplessness....

Where is the beauty? The roses, golden light and whispering water, dancing flowers, dew drops and honey pots, golden eyes peering through the branches. The smell of damp leaves in the sunshine.

Feel abandoned. Led to the rough stuff and dropped on the ground. Door slammed, key dropped, and all have run away.

I remember her in the workshop, struggling to define herself—and feeling disappointed at not having an epiphany. When she changed her room, she told us, "I added a big fat chair that felt like hope to me and a vase and flowers that felt like joy. I like the chair. It's a chair that's been around."

After reading her despairing message, I reply that no human being is one hundred percent unworthy but that feelings of unworthiness perpetuate themselves. I suggest that every day she pick one positive belief about herself and reinforce it all day, in various ways. She likes the idea. She says she feels hopeful.

"No pain, no gain," my sons used to chant during wrestling season. While deep work isn't pleasant, its rewards are usually worth the struggle. In my experience, people who successfully muscle through self-assumed inadequacies—along with those who fight the undertow of emotional resistance—benefit greatly from the work. Once they clear that obstacle course of their own making, they end up with "less pain" and "more gain" than they could possibly have imagined.

DOING IT RIGHT WHILE DOING IT WRONG

Often by "doing it wrong," some of us get exactly what we need or want. Along the path of spiritual alchemy, "doing it wrong" often translates to "doing it right."

"I can't meditate"

Nadine can't meditate. Not ever, not in any way. She's tried sitting still, watching her breath, staring at candles. Nothing works. So she can't see the point of visualizing a safe haven. It's too much like meditating—and *she can't do it*!!

As most of us in this particular workshop are meditators, we laugh. We had the same problems, we tell her. It happens to everyone. Just keep trying, one day it will work. I add that if the visualizing doesn't work for her, she should close her eyes and wait for the rest of the instructions. She doesn't have to feel bad about any of it. After all, this isn't a meditation workshop.

Later, after the exercise in rearranging the room and asking a question in it, Nadine grins sheepishly, almost lazily: "I didn't do it. I wanted to, but I sort of vanished during the energy-balancing part. I didn't hear a word you said."

"Where were you?" we want to know.

"I don't know. I just kind of 'blissed out' and vanished. No words, no sounds, no sense of time. When I heard you talking and opened my eyes, I felt cleansed."

"That's meditation!" somebody shouts, and we all start laughing. By doing it "wrong," Nadine has learned to meditate.

We cannot do it "wrong," for the simplest of reasons—one that Donna Bivens expresses best: "The soul is always waiting." No matter how long it takes us to get to our truths, no matter how circuitous the path, no matter how many obstacles we place in our own way, the soul is always waiting.

"DOING IT WRONG" BY RESISTING

The most striking form of "doing it wrong" is *resisting*. Because the various forces behind people's resistance are so powerful, and because overcoming or releasing resistance is key to the practice of spiritual alchemy, resistance demands a chapter all its own.

CHAPTER
10

Resisting the Process

In the very first workshop (attended by my friend Ruth, some friends of hers, and my mother), we all know one another or have heard good things about each other. Trust is a given. Early on, I warn everyone that resistance is possible. I explain why I value it and why they should, too. The first exercise goes smoothly, as does listing beliefs about ourselves and finding the furnishings. But as soon as I mention sketching our rooms, Ruth draws herself up and announces, "I don't want to do this!"

"Why not?"

"I don't know, and I don't care. I just don't want to!"

RESISTING

Resistance, like a slinky or a snake, can take many forms. Sometimes a single simple exercise can trigger waves of resistance in an otherwise receptive person. Sometimes a person's feelings of inadequacy mask themselves as resistance. Still other people approach the workshop with chips on their shoulders, wanting something valuable to happen while unconsciously or consciously sabotaging the process.

The simplest kind of resistance develops around only one exercise. That exercise triggers the resistance, no differently from wheat or strawberries triggering an allergic reaction. Unlike food sensitivities, however, if we acknowledge and push through the resistance, we are likely to never have to suffer from that particular sensitivity again.

Ruth has the self-awareness not to stop at "I don't want to." She immediately adds, "I can feel the resistance rising. I know I promised you I'd do everything, so I'll make myself do it, but I don't want to!"

She grins: "Oh, it feels good to be able to say 'I don't want to' and not have to defend myself. And I'm really curious to find out why I'm so resistant to something so trivial."

Although Ruth no longer remembers what triggered her resistance, she thinks she was daunted by the organizing involved in creating a room: all those pieces of furnishings, all that drawing, all that *planning*. As a self-defined "disorganized" person, she hated the prospect of doing the work. By the next morning, however, she had drawn, cut out, and pasted onto paper an entire roomful of items—and reported with well-deserved pride that the organizing itself had taken her only ten minutes.

Ruth's clarity, honesty, and ability to laugh at herself have become a benchmark for me as I help others work through their resistance. Although very few people are clear about their resistance, remembering Ruth's breakthrough is a steady reminder of the rewards we all can reap from overcoming resistance.

"I CAN'T SEE THE VALUE"

Belinda balks at the thought of arranging lists. She is a thoughtful, spiritual African-American woman with years of experience in consciousness raising, processing, and group dynamics. Under no circumstances, she insists, will she make lists.

"Lists are linear. I've spent too many years unlearning linear thinking and linear processing for me to see any value in doing it now. I'm not trying to be resistant, but I can't see the value in this exercise and don't want to do it."

Looking into her clear eyes, I feel total respect for her honesty. From her perspective, she isn't resisting the work; she's simply speaking her heartfelt truth.

"Belinda," I say, "I'm not going to argue with you. If you don't want to do it, don't."

"But I need to understand why you think this exercise is valuable, when I see it as reactionary. I think it's taking us back in the wrong direction. I can't see what it has to do with anything spiritual!"

"And I need you to understand why you're reacting so strongly. After all, it's just an exercise. It's harmless, it can't hurt you. But your resistance is like a mother lode of gold. Why don't you mine it for all it's worth?"

"Doing linear work," she insists, "goes against the grain of everything I've worked so hard to become." After continuing in that vein for a few minutes, she pauses. "And yet... you're right, I need to know why I'm fighting it so hard."

"If you can say that, you're halfway there. Go for it. What are you afraid of?"

"I don't think I'm afraid, and I think I know myself pretty well. But I'm willing to take a look at it." She takes a few deep breaths, and we continue the dialogue. Suddenly she lets out a huge sigh and sits up straight.

"I've got it. It is fear. Fear that if I do the exercise, I'll go back to being who I used to be. Fear that I might not really be the strong, liberated person I thought I was. Otherwise, I wouldn't be afraid of the exercise. I still have more work to do on myself."

"I think you've just done it," someone says, looking at Belinda in awe.

"Whew," she beams. "I don't have to fear anymore that one little exercise in linearity will undo a lifetime's worth of work. I can trust my changes. I can honor my growth and self-worth."

Both Ruth and Belinda offer positive models for working with resistance. Because they so clearly acknowledged their resistance, it didn't overwhelm them. Use their examples as guideposts if resistance ever gets the better of you.

Cultural interference

Some resistance is cultural, especially in areas of the country where people do not commonly meet people very different from themselves. My father used to tell a story about working on a construction project in Hope, Arkansas, in the early 1940s. A woman he was dating brought him home to meet her mother and mentioned that he was Jewish.

"But he looks just like us!" the mother exclaimed. My father always laughed when remembering his date's embarrassment, as she explained to her mother that Jews didn't have horns on their heads or tails on their behinds.

Although my father's story may sound extreme, ignorance of other cultures can lead to cultural interference—and straight to resistance. So can being taught—and still believing—that your culture or religion is the only "true" one and that all others are tainted or dangerous.

Janet comes up to me during a break. With her sweet, open face, she strikes me as a woman who never makes waves and never wants to hurt anyone's feelings. She likes the process, she says, but the chakra-balancing we did before one of the exercises makes her uneasy. I tell her it's just a warm-up tool that she can skip if she wants. But she insists on knowing more: "Isn't it part of another religion?"

As we are in the Bible Belt, I guess that Janet is worried that chakras belong to a non-Christian religion. I ask her if she knows about acupuncture, about the use of the body's natural energy system for preventing or stopping pain. She has. I tell her that lots of Western doctors are now using acupuncture in their daily practice, and that chakras are something like acupuncture points. In Eastern medicine, they are simply a way of understanding energy flow in the body—and that all we are doing is physically balancing our natural, God-given energies.

Janet's face brightens. "Oh, if that's all it is, I can do it. I just didn't want to do something my pastor would disapprove of."

bundled into heavy sweaters and jackets. (Later we learn that on a major lakefront in mid-November, the building management was turning off the heat on weekends!)

The first person to discuss her experience sits on Candace's left. His experience is so rich and meaningful that I have the sharing move around the circle in the opposite direction, leaving Candace for last. Whether listening or not, by now she is hunched into an almost fetal position.

"Candace?"

Silence. Then: "I guess I'm still different. I didn't have any questions to ask, like everybody else. I just sat there in the meditation, until a question sort of came." She pauses, straightening slightly. "I guess I can read it."

Suddenly, as if from out of nowhere, a high-pitched, plaintive child's voice fills the room, crying, "Where is my daddy?"

We sit stunned, staring, as Candace curls back into herself, wracked with silent sobs. She finally gulps, inhales sharply, and says she wants to continue. "I told you I was different," she whispers. "Even my answer doesn't sound like any of yours."

> Where is my daddy?
>
> Your daddy is in the heart of God. Where else would you seek for him, my love? You are not lost. Merely come home to me and I will give you peace and make you warm and safe. There is no safety elsewhere. Why would you seek for it where it is not? I have told you this over and over, yet you do not hear, seeking for peace where it is not. Bob has no peace, you cannot find it in him, much as you may want to. He, too, looks for it where it is not. Go back to your readings. They brought to you the peace you seek. Know that you are on the right path. And it is good. And it has heart. And it is the way to the truth and the light. He who believes in me will never die.

No one moves or speaks. Eventually, after honoring Candace's courage, I say the obvious: that this clear voice—in short sentences and simple words—is the soul voice. This is what it sounds like, this is how it presents itself.

Candace also shares with us her message from the final exercise, in a voice no longer distant. When I pick up the mailing list, her name is on it.

I think of her from time to time, wishing her well in her search for her missing, absent, or long-dead father. A year later, I send out my first letter asking participants if they wish to contribute to this book. I am amazed to receive from Candace a long response that shatters my earlier speculations about her father.

Here is Candace's letter nearly in full. Her story does more than exemplify the basic fear of "doing it wrong." It also shows what caused the fear—and the damage from both the original cause and the resulting fear. In honor of her requests, I have not quoted her out of context and have changed the names and a few minor details.

The answer to "Where is my daddy?" was most significant for me. My father was (and still is) a quiet man, logical and precise in his thinking, an engineer by trade. Emotions had no place in the home I grew up in—or should I say, were looked down upon and undefined. No words for *mad sad glad afraid ashamed hurt*. The closest I came to identifying shame in my 20's was to realize that **I felt foolish** most of the time, without knowing why. If anyone spoke in our home, the validity or accuracy was challenged by my father's skeptical, "Is that right?" So we learned to defend our "rights" and "wrongs," learned to value a win-lose scenario, learned to make sure we had our "footnotes," our sources, our "proof" handy for all that we said. Learned, in short, to doubt ourselves and our reality, deeply.

Contempt and disdain were the unspoken masters at home. Disdain for the lesser (perceived) intelligence of others. The Millers were and ARE, if nothing else, intelligent. And very afraid of being perceived as stupid (i.e., ashamed).

My father was sometimes vicious in his contempt. I remember his face, skewed in rage, spitting out words I no longer recall. But I remember the face, and the pain his disdain caused. I always wanted to do something good enough to win his approval; I always heard that what I wanted to do didn't measure up.

"Why do you want to do THAT? Artists don't make any money. Why do you want to learn Chinese?"

I tried to conform to what I thought he wanted. I gave up my dreams. I died and died and died, a little at a time, until I no longer tried. I became a cynic, condemning others for their foolishness, their stupidity, their faults. I became my father.

At times, I walked around with the proverbial chip on my shoulder, mentally daring people to brush it off. I walked into your seminar that way. Teach me something I don't already know, I challenged. You took the challenge, and in doing so, earned my respect.

I am not, was not, new to emotional or spiritual work. I've done plenty of both. Just didn't trust it yet (I'd learned the RULES very well). I've stood in heaven more times than I can count, and while I feel blessed that this is true, it's also true that nothing less would convince me it exists. I'm a tough teach.

I don't remember exactly the instructions which led me to write what I did. I remember being asked to ask a question of the sacred room we had created for ourselves. I remember asking for the "right" question to be given to me, since I did not seem able to come up with (or perhaps, narrow down) a question on my own.

The question, "where is my daddy," has been a recurring one for me throughout therapy in recent years and throughout the mental/spiritual work I have done. It did not occur to me that the question actually had, or needed, an answer. It would come up in association with seeing my father's face, filled with rage and contempt. "Where is my daddy? You're not my daddy." That is, you're not the kind, gentle, loving daddy I think of as MY daddy. The aspect of my personality experiencing the memory of the face and the inevitable accompanying questions was quite vulnerable, so I tend to think of that aspect as young or as a child.

I believe that painful experiences are repeated or re-experienced until the soul can heal them, after which the experience is resolved and no longer presents itself.

Such is the case with my question. I no longer see my father's rage-filled face, no longer experience the shame associated with it, no longer ask the question. The question has been answered.

In like ways, the heart chakra/third eye meditation was helpful/reassuring. I need to read from time to time that the man I love, on the highest level, loves me and IS there for me, that I can trust him, that he'll always be there for me.

These are things I need to come back to, to remind myself that the level of soul and spirit and God is REAL and holds ALL of the answers we seek. It has taken me a long time to trust that, AND know that my life is easier and works better when I do trust it.

....Currently I am traveling across the country meeting people, learning about myself, and discovering what might be the next step for me in God's plan. In short, I am practicing **following my heart**, in direct contrast to what I feel I learned growing up. It takes, more than anything, surrender and trust, and the more I practice these, the more inclined I am to practice them, as they seem to lead me down THE GOOD ROAD, whatever that is.

I expect I will send a copy of this to my dad, and possibly to Bob. Please change our family name if you should use this, for the sake of my dad. And I pray that he will understand that what I have written is not REAL-ITY carved in STONE, but **my** truth as I PERCEIVED it, or as I remember it, and that for some reason **independent** of him, it was important for me along MY path to remember and experience these things this way. (I love you, Dad. I always have.)

RESISTING CHANGE

The most subtle form of resistance I've encountered has nothing to do with the exercises. Instead, it is an unconscious response to the difficult changes we all need to make at major crossroads in our lives. Most of us, myself included, go kicking and screaming into our changes. We often end up with life crises that force us into those changes, whether we want them or not. If we are honest with ourselves, we realize that resisting change will lead us down a dead-end street, while facing or embracing change will reveal a path to new insights, growth, and joy.

Participants who resist inner changes rarely resist the exercises themselves. The resistance in these people is so deep and hidden that they remain unaware of resisting anything. But, somehow, something goes "wrong" in an exercise, and the true nature of the hidden resistance surfaces. Whether they grow from the experience—whether they use what they uncover—depends on them.

"The wise one"

Barbara was a middle-aged psychotherapist in private practice. *Was*, because she has recently retired. She is finally writing the novel that she has been researching and obsessing over for years. Excited about her work, she is at the International Women's Writing Guild conference, where professional criticism, good writing, and general enthusiasm abound. Now, she feels, she will have a chance to share her passion with people who understand writing and can help her with her book.

She never tells me why she chooses my workshop among the several she takes. She says she has a hunch I might know something about her topic. I do, and that seals the bond.

The group is large. I have never before had 60 people all wanting to talk at once, and I feel overwhelmed by their creativity and insights. By the final exercise, I see in their faces the question, "How can she top what happened yesterday? What's coming next?"

I walk them through the chakra-balancing meditation, then have them focus on their heart chakra, concentrating on feelings of gratitude, appreciation, and love. After five minutes, I ask them to let the energy soar "to your third eye."

They come out of their altered states in stages. Soon everyone is writing. Some are sobbing. I walk around the room, putting out emotional fires. "Are you okay?" I ask each one. Almost everyone says "yes"; these are tears of joy for revelations, powerful meditative experiences, uncanny visions. But Barbara is not okay. Her tear-streaked face is lined with pain, aging her ten years. I ask her if she can wait until everyone finishes writing. She nods.

During the discussion period, hands shoot up. People read inspiring, illuminating descriptions of what they heard or saw. Then Barbara raises her hand. "I don't want to be a wet blanket, but I had a disturbing experience."

"What happened?"

"Well, I was fairly comfortable in my heart, though I mostly thought about all the people I've known who have died, and how even though I love them, they're not in my life anymore. Then, when you told us to go to our head, I got the following message":

The fullness of time has come and gone

Death stalks

Creating darkness

Soon, soon he will come

Finish

Be ready

I ask her how she feels.

"Terrible. I'm not ready to die."

Her pain is so palpable, I feel terrible, too. But I also trust her soul.

"Are you certain it means that you're going to die?"

"It was from the Grim Reaper. Who else?"

I ponder this briefly, feeling caught between her needing help and the others needing to return to their joyfulness. "It's not like the soul voice to give this kind of a message," I tell her, "so the meaning may be different from what you think. Do you think you can hang in there for a bit, until we can talk later?"

She nods, and we go on. I silently ask for an answer to surface. When the session ends, I say to her, "I think I know the problem. You gave me the clue when you said 'go to our head.' I think you went to your head—your fears—and not to your third eye."

But she is already smiling. "I got another line. It all makes sense now."

She explains it later:

My inner response [on getting the message] was profound. Tears started slowly at the "Death stalks" line and became an open floodgate by "Be ready." I was certain I was receiving a message of my imminent death...a devastating message.

The last line—my answer—came, unbidden, some minutes later: "It is hard to give up being the wise one." It was the message for which I was to "Be ready"; it was the death that stalked me.

Evidently, my retirement as a psychotherapist was not as well integrated as I thought. I have to go through the death of that part of me, that role— grieve for it, then lay it to rest. For so many years I was "the wise one." I carried inside me the lives of so many people, their concerns and their tragedies. I struggled alongside each one as we fought together to change them. In meeting them at their vision of reality and shifting it, I watched many deaths in my office. Now it happened to me.

If I wrap myself in the role of PSYCHOLOGIST for the rest of my life, if I freeze into it, the great Self, the Creative Self, will be blocked. My writing will be too ego-oriented, too academic, too controlled by the fear of disapproval, too small.

I heard them there, the women who had surrendered the ego to allow being open to the Creative Self. Their work was lush, deep, open.... I want that. It is my heart's desire. So I must let that other part of me die.

Your workshop opened the way, and the Creative Self came.

I run into Barbara the next day after breakfast. She is beaming. Not only has she shed the ten years of pain, she looks ten years younger than that. She has been looking for me, to tell me her news. She has found a professional editor to help her with her book, she has discovered her "Creative Self," and she is free to "die." She is becoming a spiritual alchemist.

A few years later I read the opening chapter of her first book. Gone is the academic voice. In its place stands an intriguing story line and vibrant language. We begin corresponding. I observe that in letting the "wise one" die, she shed only the role. She herself has become wise.

11

Repeating the Process
The Second (Third, Fourth) Time Around....

A fter creating their room, most people believe that they will either (a) use it forever, exactly as it is, because it's perfect; (b) keep redecorating until it's perfect; or (c) need to clean it out and refurnish it until it's perfect. No matter how often I suggest that the room is likely to change as we grow, few people believe me—especially those who love their rooms. No matter how much we want to become spiritual alchemists, to continue the life-long process of spiritual and emotional individuation, the human habit of looking for "something that works" and then sticking to it (rather than growing with or from it) is hard to break.

But alchemy involves the continual balancing of opposites, which change as we change, as does our shadow. Therefore, as we grow, we need to be aware of the changes in our shadow, so that we can acknowledge and incorporate them into our lives—and into our inner laboratory. Not surprisingly, in his major work on alchemy (*Mysterium Coniunctionis*), Carl Jung likened an individual's "coming to terms with" his or her own shadow to the alchemist's *unio mentalis*—the union of spirit and soul:

"The *unio mentalis*..., in psychological as well as alchemical language, means knowledge of oneself."

In continuing to work with your room, always remember that every one of its furnishings is a symbol. Each one symbolizes a deeply held belief of yours—and each contains all the power that accompanies any symbol. As Jung wrote, "What the alchemist sought...to help him out of his dilemma was a chemical operation which we today would describe as a symbol." He continued with a "recipe" for the best use of that symbol. As you read it, think of your laboratory:

Take the unconscious in one of its handiest forms, say a spontaneous fantasy, a dream, an irrational mood...and operate with it. Give it your special attention, concentrate on it, and observe its alterations objectively. Spare no effort to devote yourself to this task, follow the subsequent transformations...attentively and carefully. Above all, don't let anything from outside, that does not belong, get into it, for the fantasy-image has "everything it needs." In this way one is certain of not interfering by conscious caprice and of giving the unconscious a free hand.

This chapter gives you several "users' reports"—a peek into the "special attention" of several people who have taken the workshop twice or more. In small ways and large, these repeat participants will walk you through their process of reconstructing the room. In some cases, their new room did exactly what it was supposed to do—and the joke was on them.

Carol Reiff, taking the workshop a second time, told everyone how much she was enjoying *purposely* designing her room without thinking about what the pieces stood for. Everything was delightfully falling into place, she said, except for a grandfather clock.

Suddenly I started getting crazed: "Should I put it over here? over there? in this corner? in that? No, it won't fit there—what about this corner?" I began obsessing about it, driving myself nuts. Finally I couldn't stand the tension anymore, so I turned back the page to see what the clock stood for—and it turned out to be *obsessive*!

REARRANGING

Often, the best new insights come from naming, arranging, and *rearranging* the room whenever necessary. Many returning participants tell me that the changes in their rooms, more than anything else, become their benchmarks for measuring their growth.

The second time around, Genie tells me, "I find the room a wonderful safe haven to which I may return. I like the amount of thoughtfulness needed to 'name, arrange, and pattern.' It is no quick fix, no easy excuse."

She writes in her journal:

I enjoy transforming my beliefs into concrete objects that can be placed in a room. I notice that my room is similar to the one I did last year, but has some differences. There are some new items: a toilet (for menopause) and a large cleaver (for RESENTMENT). The cleaver disturbs me a bit, so I contemplate the meaning of it, coming up with this: "As I walk around the campus [where the workshop is taking place] I see that I RESENT not having enough time for myself. If I have ENOUGH time for myself, I love to be loving and helpful. Then I can use the cleaver to CARVE OUT time for myself."

Later in the workshop I use Natalie's idea of the knife for protection. My cleaver or knife can serve double duty, to cut and to protect....

When we return to the room, I am pleased to use what we have learned to transform some of the items. I transform the toilet into a bubbling fountain next to a plant. I add pieces of myself that seemed to be missing, such as a thick rug for yoga and a music player by the hammock. My desk no longer represents my propensity for messiness, it is just for writing. Most important is the transformation of the cleaver.

Genie doesn't demand that the room stay the same as the year before; she allows who she is now to determine what goes in it. Although both menopause and resentment entered her room as negative items, she transforms them into positives by recognizing their true function in her life.

Other people notice that the room itself—as if it had a will of its own—will make the changes it needs. Paula Mate comments that her *angry* drainboard became the *evil* drainboard when it moved from her list into the drawing. "I let the change stand," she said. "I figured it had morphed." Allowing herself to accept the wisdom of her unconscious word switch, Paula lets the room decide what it needs to be—and lets the room be her teacher.

Paula also notices that when she questions her feelings, she finds major items in her room remaining from workshop to workshop—but with their meanings changed.

In my first drawing of the room, I had the *jealous* molding around the *envious* French doors, leading out to the *grateful* porch. (I had recently put a porch on my house that I was grateful for, that had been motivated by a good envy, that is, asking why couldn't I have something that other people had [when an architect and a builder and a husband all kept telling me it wouldn't work out—but it did, and it's beautiful].)

I also made a marginal note about the envious French doors: "Is part of the good envy (that makes us move toward getting what we want) something I can be grateful for?" I saw that the envious French doors became the *gratitude* doors when I allowed myself to open to what I wanted.

Paula's questioning and reframing her envy, first as "good envy" and later as "gratitude," allowed her to keep both her doors and her porch, all in a positive way.

A PERSONAL BENCHMARK

After her second workshop, one year after the first, biologist Marion Perkus observed that "halfway into an exercise, I would remember what it was leading up to, then just let the knowledge go. The 'same but not the same' emphasized for me just how much my concerns and focus have changed over the past year."

After a third workshop, she added: "It was interesting to me, doing the room three distinct times with intervals of about a year each. In the repeats, there was a dim sense of remembering bits and pieces of the previous time(s). This gave me a benchmark for seeing how my room, my preoccupations, and overall sense of myself had changed."

The changes in Marion are profound. Her first room is quiet and peaceful, with a theme of both shallow and deep water running through it:

> My meditation cushion (*at peace*) is flanked on the left by a fireplace with embers (*full of hidden anger*) and on the right by plants (*in process of healing*). I look out over a goldfish pool (*tranquil on surface*) and look past it through a large clear window (*Vajra*) at the back of the room. In front of me water flows from my right from a deep well or pool which is the source of water (*tranquil in depths*), through the shallow, sunlit pool (*tranquil on surface*). There is an underground water connection all along the left side of the room....

By the following year, her imagery has dramatically changed:

> The basic shape of the room is a soundproofed *quiet* semicircle arching around a large picture window with muted, slightly drawn curtains.
>
> The desk (*financial security*) supports *generosity, observant, expressive, intelligent, remembers, hard to let go of memory*. All are illumined by the gooseneck lamp of *questing*.
>
> The mirror (*introspective*) is withdrawn, at the very back of the room.
>
> *Light* and *timid* are illumined by sunlight coming through the open window. All are reflected in the mirror of introspection.
>
> My "waiting room" (*patient)* is invisible, just a floating space that hovers in the middle—a space for *soft, compassionate, sensitive,* and *avoiding conflict* to congregate and hover.

windows (*not as good a listener as I'd like to be*). I have several lampshades (*sensitive*) but no lamps! A large throw rug (*too quick to anger*) sits in front of a bookcase (*teacher*), which supports a religious icon (*wanting to do good*). A coffee table (*good parent*) faces a sofa (*needs improvement*). Over the sofa hangs a Japanese silkscreen print (*compassionate*). A hammock (*lacking discipline*) hangs over a *hope* chest. A windchime (*impatient*) hangs by one window. There is no door.

Although I can find only two patterning notes from that first day, they are telling:

- *Lacking discipline* is hanging over *hope*.
- I need to add some lamps for *it's OK that I'm not perfect* and put some *sensitivity* lampshades over them.

FIRST MAJOR CHANGE

My inner laboratory remains rectangular through the fourth workshop, in which a wonderfully artistic participant shows us her drawing of an oval room with curved spaces and spirals throughout. I see that I've been thinking "inside the box." I realize that I don't have to have a box, nor do I want to rely on a familiarly shaped European-style room. From that day forward, my room becomes a circle.

A few workshops into my circular room, I find myself arranging my list of names in spirals. I write: "I think time moves in spirals. My room is an introduction to the meaning of time."

SETTLING IN

By 1999, my inner laboratory has taken on a familiar shape, with certain consistent furnishings. A circular mandala, it has four picture windows at the cardinal directions and faces west onto the ocean, with a telescope and an observatory roof. A spiral staircase leads down to the beach.

The room almost always contains a central spiral staircase leading up to a sleeping loft with a bed, near the observatory window. It often has a desk and chair facing the ocean, a sofa with cushions under one window, a bookcase between two windows, and a heavy oak work table. All of these furnishings—plus the various items on the walls, desk, table, and bookcase—vary in meaning, depending on where I am in my life.

In other words, over time, much of the room has become familiar—not static, but familiar. The room works for me. We know one another. The major pieces, the major qualities, the major beliefs are part of me—or so I think. I am aware that my needs change, depending on the issues or priorities facing me, and the feelings I have towards dealing with them. I feel settled but flexible.

I have no clue what's coming.

PATTERNING AND INSIGHTS OVER FOUR WORKSHOPS

The following patterning notes will give you a glimpse into the power of the room over time. The power of knowing yourself, free of the opinions of others, free of outside tools. The power of patterning in the room itself. The power of having an inner laboratory for conducting spiritual alchemy—and of *being* a spiritual alchemist.

To show you the incredible wisdom that comes from frequent patterning, I'm going to give you a shortened version of my patterning notes around *one* event in the fall of 1999. All the background you need is that the previous December, my beloved father had died, and in August my then-husband had demanded a divorce.

The event is cancer.

Because I write a lot when I'm patterning, I'm including only a few highlights for each of the four occasions, followed by a summarizing paragraph called "looking back." If you like the brevity and focus of the *looking back* paragraphs, you might want to return after weeks or months to your own patterning notes and create *looking back* paragraphs of your own. As you'll soon see, the process is richly illuminating.

Patterning notes, October 1999—shortly after I have moved out of my house and a few weeks before I get a diagnosis of uterine cancer

- *Compassionate* (*thanka* of Avalokiteshvara, Buddha of compassion) balances *telepathic* (Australian aboriginal painting)
- Being *boundaried* (door) and *protected* (death mask) allows me freedom!
- My being *loving* (couch) supports *befriended* (cushions).
- *Stress* (frayed carpet edges) frays the edges of my being *centered* (Persian carpet).
- Warm liquids in a mug made by a friend (*self-nurturing*) protect me from danger from the burning candle (*spewing out last vestiges of rage*).
- *Analytical, productive* & *creative* face west, the direction of death and rebirth.

Looking back

Exhausted without knowing why, I create a room that reflects the illness and predicts the future: Being **stressed** has thrown my immune system off balance. **Self-nurturing** will help me heal from the **danger** that my **spewing rage** is causing. My being **befriended**, because I had been **loving**, saves my life: Friends take me in, care for me, pray for me. The entire cancer episode opens me more fully to **compassion**, balancing my over-valuing my **telepathic** gifts. **Death** is coming to my **analytical, productive**, and **creative** sides, all of which essentially vanish into "chemo-brain" until my treatment ends. **Rebirth** follows treatment.

Patterning notes, early November 1999—one week after the diagnosis, with the probability of a large ovarian malignancy

- No meditation chair, no desk chair, no chairs. A lamp and a mirror. A time to stand on my own feet and really look at myself.
- No *soft*, *analytical*, or *intellectual*. Time to be strong about getting out of my head!
- I need to be *grounded* (wood floor) to be *compassionate* (large Persian carpet). *Connection to the divine* (observatory window) *enlightens compassion.*
- My being *too much in my personality* (Bobo the clown) stands in the way of being *divinely connected* (a *shviti*, a Jewish religious wall hanging).
- Nothing is in the East, the place of new beginnings.

Looking back

Once I know I have cancer, the room changes. I know I have to **stand on my own two feet, get out of my head**, and **look at myself**—and be **strong** about it. My feelings of being **protected** are no longer **grounded**—and I needed to be both grounded and **connected to the divine** to be **compassionate** with myself and others. I need both **creativity** and **courage** to face the **dark** (my shadow side), because **being too much in my personality** (my usual way of interacting with people) is blocking my ability to interact with the divine. Feeling **valued** is my only doorway in and out of that hard work. Nothing in my life is the same. Everything is new.

Patterning notes, late November 1999—one week later, four days after periodontal surgery and ten days before a radical hysterectomy

- My spiral staircases are reversed!
- *Analytical* and *insightful* sit on the floor, below *intuitive* (meditation chair), which faces through *openness* (window) into *deep spirituality* (ocean). It is the death of analysis and insight as I have known them. Being intuitive is the key.

Looking back

Certain themes remain, such as the need for balancing **judgmentalism** and intellectual snobbery with **compassion**. But now the desk is gone, with my old ideas about **analytical** and **insightful** temporarily out of commission. I can't think, let alone have insights or work, in the middle of medical tests, each more scary than the next. Facing surgery, I am learning to **reverse** the direction of my life—to come **up** from the **deeply spiritual**, to start in the **depths** of my fears. I can no longer rely on old behavior patterns. They are on the floor. All I have left is my **intuition**—which is telling me to go into the depths, to start my work at the bottom.

Typing these words for this book, I noticed that in 1999 I completely overlooked the crucial differences between *analysis*, *insight*, and *intuition*. My "well-educated, analytical" mind knew that *analysis* means "taking apart," *insight* means "looking in(to)," and *intuition* means "inward knowing." So I was clearly capable then of realizing that analysis involves a form of *acting*, that insight involves a form of *seeing*, and that intuition involves a form of *knowing*.

But redoing and repatterning my room brought these distinctions to life in a way that logical analysis never did. In my laboratory that day in 1999, analysis and insight sat **below** intuition, **at the feet of** intuition. Surgery and who-knows-what-else was coming. Gone was the time of acting or seeing. All I had left was an **inner knowing** that faced **deeply spiritual**—and to which I had to be **open** and **receptive**.

Patterning notes, April 2000—a month after the last chemotherapy treatment and two days before radiation treatment starts

- Nothing sits on the bookcase. Being *knowledgeable* no longer supports anything.
- Forms of "letting go" are at all the *open* windows. I am open to heart and to *fear-shedding*.
- I "accidentally" got my directions confused and put my *shviti* [which is supposed to face east towards Jerusalem] in the North, facing the dark. I am *protected* as long as I face my shadow.
- Only by being joyous and self-aware can I go out of myself and go to the depths.
- *Seeking wisdom* (telescope) is what allows me to stay *connected to the divine* (observatory roof).
- *Willingness to work hard* (desk) supports *intuitive, analytical,* and *self-nurturing*.

Looking back

Integration, not education, is the key. I no longer live in my head, though I don't need to deny its strengths. Although **analytical** is back, it is in balance with **intuitive** and **self-nurturing**. Gone is the arrogance of considering myself far-seeing; the telescope has become **wisdom-seeking**. Gone is the arrogance of being **knowledgeable**: Cancer has taught me that life isn't fair, that no amount of green tea, vitamins, or meditation will make me live forever. My real protection is internal—through facing my shadow. The only **connection to the divine** is through **seeking wisdom**. The only way to the **depths** is through **joy** and **self-awareness**. Most importantly, the process of **integrating** these qualities is forever ongoing.

A few new beliefs appear on every list I make, sometimes replacing old ones, sometimes not. This April 2000 list, however, had over 15 new beliefs, including *willing to learn, wisdom-seeking, whole-self-embracing, fierce, implacable, flexible, integrating, woman-in-waiting*, and *fear-shedding*. While I would never have chosen cancer as my teacher, redoing my room clearly showed me how much I was learning.

As I reread this last *looking back* paragraph, I see in it all the hallmarks of the spiritual alchemist:

> My real protection is internal—through facing my shadow. The only connection to the divine is through seeking wisdom. The only way to the depths is through joy and self-awareness. Most importantly, the process of integrating these qualities is forever ongoing.

These basic insights and perspectives characterized the ancient alchemists and characterize all spiritual alchemists everywhere. Through your own experiences, both in your inner laboratory and elsewhere, you will find your own words and your own way of framing these same key understandings: The process never ends. Joy can go hand-in-glove with self-awareness if that awareness is authentic. And wisdom-seeking through facing yourself (shadow and all) will connect you profoundly with the divine.

KEYS TO YOUR INNER LABORATORY

These "users' reports" all point to the value of working in your inner laboratory and understanding the power of the furnishings as symbols. The longer you work in—and with—your room, the more you will learn about yourself. As Carl Jung wrote, *"A symbol does not disguise, it reveals in time."* [italics his]

The following chapter will show you how to work with your room in new ways, so that the deeper meanings of your furnishings "reveal" themselves "in time." ⚷

CHAPTER
12

Continuing the Journey

Whenever I get confused, I take my emotional temperature by doing my room
—Paula Mate

The workshop is over, the exercises done.
"Go to your room and work with it," I urge everyone. "The laboratory is yours, whenever you need it. Go there often to do deep spiritual alchemy, to commune with your soul, find your life's purpose, get ideas and inspiration for all types of creative work. It is—and it contains—the core of who you are. It will change as you change, so go there often and use it."

Some people do. But many, I suspect, don't. The intensity and clarity of a good workshop experience tend to fade after a while. The momentum dies down. Daily habits take over. We remember the room and think about it, from time to time. Then we begin to forget how we created it, what we were supposed to do in it. And where did our notes go? Somewhere in that pile of papers? Maybe thrown out? How did the instructor walk us through it? How were we supposed to balance our energies? Where's the crib sheet, now that she's not here? Oh well, it was a great workshop, even if I can't remember how to....

The same thing happens with a book like this. We plan to read it again, but errands and obligations get in the way. We loan it to someone and then forget which friend it was, so we can't ask for it back. We plan to go to our inner laboratory often, because the experience was so rich, but....

It happens to us all.

One person speaks for many when she writes to me:

I have wanted to talk with you about the process you taught us. I somehow have been able to use it fleetingly. I think I am afraid of the power it gives me. I am further surprised by my fear but I do acknowledge it. I keep telling myself I need a minimum of a 3- or 4-hour block of time to apply it and of course with my lifestyle I can't find those kind of time slots easily.

This woman is honest enough to recognize that she is afraid and that she is avoiding facing her fear. Fear keeps us from working with the soul, because we reach our soul through love, and love is the opposite of fear. When you sat in your room to work, remember how you entered in joy and gratitude? how you "sat" in your heart for five minutes? The real door to the room, as all spiritual alchemists know, is through the deeper knowing, through the heart. When your heart is full of gratitude, compassion, and love, it has no room for fear.

I reminded this woman that all she had to do was sit in her heart, and the fear would vanish. All she needed—and all that you need—is 15–20 minutes at a time...or less. As Donna Bivens said, "The soul is always waiting."

But questions remain: How can you continue working with your room, now that you've done all the exercises? Is this set of exercises all there is to becoming a spiritual alchemist? In other words, how can you continue the process you've just begun—and deepen your practice as a spiritual alchemist?

As usual, former workshop participants—and current spiritual alchemists—have some of your answers.

"A WAY OF KNOWING WHAT'S GOING ON INSIDE"

Paula Mate uses her room as "a check-in for where I am when I'm not sure of what I'm feeling." She makes a list of 10–15 "I am known as" names, and another list of "as many adjectives as come out." Once, when she ran out of adjectives for her beliefs about herself, she knew from previous "decorating" that she wanted certain items in the room. So she used them. After making the list, she wrote:

> I felt free and self-empowered enough to name the object—door, windows, lighting—and then *I found the belief **after** naming the furniture*." [italics mine]
>
> All of this helps ground me and helps me get to know an essential self I can count on. By doing this from time to time (especially when I'm feeling as if I don't have it all together), when I do the pre-work for the room, I find I can count on aspects of myself to be there—because I can name them and put them in, call them up. So I'm learning to be able to count on myself more than I could before. It's very grounding.

Paula adds that using the room has given her clarity. It's "a way of knowing what's going on inside," and "a means of creating a shift in perception and attitude." To explain what she means by creating a shift, Paula says she was once so "cranky" during a vacation that she recreated and rearranged her room twice. Using the room this way, she says, gave her more than a reality check. It gave her self-awareness. It helped her become conscious of the ways in which she needed and wanted to change her negative attitude.

What Paula did lies at the heart of spiritual alchemy. She didn't ask her negativity to permanently disappear. She didn't berate herself for feeling cranky. She didn't demand some sort of unreasonable perfection from herself. Instead, she used the tools of her trade, as a spiritual alchemist, to "become conscious" and to transmute the negativity. She turned her emotional lead into gold, without having to deny that lead was and always will be a part of her *prima materia*—the primary material that all alchemists use, the inner life material that she is forever and consciously balancing.

Paula sends me the notes she wrote for herself as a reminder of why she needs to make the laboratory a part of her daily or weekly living. They include the following:

1. Doing this exercise helps me understand and accept how my space gets filled up with charged emotions that I'm not even aware of—including the positive feelings that I can make a conscious effort to keep.

2. The mix of furnishings always changes. So I gain clarity on what feelings I'm having and accept that they will always be in flux. By moving my awareness from the unconscious to the conscious, I actually get to see what I'm feeling.

3. The exercise gives me the ability to (a) embody the process of "being with" what I am feeling and (b) minimize what I don't like. For example, being able to make some of the negatives smaller puts them in better perspective with the other facets of my self-assessment.

4. All of these actions bring unknown feelings to light and **make those feelings more manageable** in my life.

Point #4, above all, speaks to the core of spiritual alchemy—the conscious, ongoing act of holding the tensions and "managing" them. Not asking them to go away but recognizing, accepting, integrating, and managing all your feelings and beliefs, your needs and your wants, your daily reality and your dreams.

But, like everything else in your room, they are not what they seem. Each represents a quality or trait that you would like to develop or strengthen in yourself. You know the quality of each before you bring it in. Turn your experience with each of these special items into a ritual. Meditate on the orchid and imagine yourself serene. Savor the water and experience yourself as flowing over or around all difficulties. Sip the champagne and feel what it feels like to be effervescent, no longer a wallflower. Smell the rose and become beautiful. Taste the caviar and know what it's like to be exotic...or worldly...or....

Only you can know what to bring, because only you can know both the quality and its appropriate symbol. If you need help in choosing the perishables or in letting them go at party's end, ask your soul for guidance.

Go joyously to this party in your room. As you try on new ways of being, know that the sip, the smell, the taste is enough for now. Remember that, like Cinderella's coach and finery, they will disappear at the stroke of midnight.

The good news is that you will now have experienced these qualities, however briefly, within the laboratory—that is, within yourself. You will have already begun to invite them in. Afterwards, allow them to come and go as they please, until they are ready to join you.

An Art Gallery

If you want to be creative in your room, then turn it into an art gallery. Or if you are a writer rather than a visual artist, make it a library—or create an art gallery by hanging magical pages from your favorite books (including, of course, your own—past, in process, or future). Think of your favorite painters, sculptors, architects, photographers, writers. Think of which paintings, sculptures, blueprints, or photographs you would like on your walls—the ones from the museums and private galleries, the ones that you could never afford to own.

For one day, turn your room into an art gallery. If it doesn't have enough space for all the art you want, then temporarily enlarge it, the way people put huge rental tents on their back lawns for weddings or special parties. Perhaps, to make space, you need to temporarily loan some of the other items in your room to a good friend. Perhaps you already have enough wall space or need only one wall. Or perhaps you can create an add-on closet to magically store other items for this one-day show.

Whatever choice you make, fill your gallery space with the art you love most. Again, know that each piece represents a quality or talent that you would like to develop or expand. Walk slowly through your room, feasting on great art and allowing it to be your teacher. You may even want to add photos or self-portraits of these artists, who may surprise you by having something to tell you.

Enjoy your wonderful collection. Be sure to make the most of the experience, because at midnight, the art will instantly return home. How deeply you let it enrich you during its one-day sojourn in your room depends on you.

Other Day-trips

You've got the idea by now. You can turn your room into a symphony hall, a darkroom, a dance hall, a potter's studio. You can, as a friend of mine has done in her home, replicate a famous writer's study and work in it for the day. As long as you confine these parties or art shows to only one day, you're home free.

The purpose of limiting this radical room-changing time is to remain true to yourself and to your journey as a spiritual alchemist. These day-long excursions are like trips to the wine country, especially when you're driving: They are for tasting, not guzzling. Like trying on clothes you can't afford today but hope to in the future, these are qualities to which you aspire. If you keep these symbolic aspirations in your room past their one-day life span, you run the risk of believing that you've become what you aren't yet. Stay true to yourself. Cultivate the patience that underlies all true alchemical processes. And always, always, ask your soul for guidance.

BALANCING BEGINNINGS AND ENDINGS

Now it is my turn to thank you. You have come to this book with an open heart, in hopes that you and your searching soul will find one another. In hopes that doing these exercises will bring you profoundly home to your very individual self. In hopes of learning to hear, and follow, the voice of your soul. In hopes of learning to become the spiritual alchemist in your own life, now and forever.

If you have done the exercises while reading the book, your laboratory—your room—is now fully outfitted and ready to go. All I have done is present the concept: from now on, from the floor plan through all future remodeling, the room is yours. It always was, it always will be. It is your home and your haven, the inner place where you in this lifetime meet and commune with your larger soul. It is your laboratory for pursuing the art and the science of spiritual alchemy. It is your touchstone, your benchmark, for your progress on the journey. For you now know, as a spiritual alchemist, that true alchemy lies both in the journey and in your commitment to it.

May the expression "go to your room!" have new meaning in your life. May you go there often and listen well. May the voice you seek be clear to you. May your practice of spiritual alchemy deepen and flourish. May you love the complex self you are learning to balance. May the journey excite you. May you continue to be a committed spiritual alchemist for the rest of your life—and may your practice and your journey bring you truly and fully home to yourself. ⚓

GUIDED

VISUALIZATIONS

This section contains all the instructions that are on the Guided Visualizations CD. Use them to refresh your memory when you're not able to play the CD.

EXERCISE 5

1. With your eyes closed, picture a quiet, peaceful place in nature, where you feel completely safe. It may be a mountaintop, a secluded beach, a forest glen, a desert cave—anywhere you choose where you feel completely safe. Think of this place as your safe haven.

2. Place yourself in this safe haven now. Hear the sounds...become aware of the smells... notice the quality of the light in your safe haven.

3. As you sit in your safe haven, think of all the many qualities that human beings share. (For example, people can be kind, generous, noisy, talkative, aggressive, peaceful, and so on. There are so many ways that people can be.)

4. With your eyes still closed, picture yourself sitting or standing in your safe haven, as if you are outside of yourself.

5. As you look at yourself, you realize that you know yourself very well. Because you do, you know what *your* dominant quality is. Quickly name—or hear the name of—your dominant quality. Then open your eyes.

> *Helpful Hint*
>
> Don't "think" about your dominant quality. The one that you hear in the exercise, the one that comes to you, may be very different from what you expect. Whether what you hear is accurate or not doesn't matter. Whatever comes to you in your safe haven is the right quality for this exercise.

6. Write down the dominant quality that you heard, knew, or thought in your safe haven.

7. Below that quality, write down its ***opposite***—the first word that comes to mind. Whatever you hear first is the right word for this exercise.

8. Now pick a situation of ***minor*** tension in your life—something annoying or irritating (but not life-threatening or overwhelming).

9. For perhaps half a minute, think about how you are handling the situation now, given your "dominant" quality.

10. Close your eyes again.

Continued on next page

11. In your mind, hand the problem or situation over to someone with that "opposite" quality you just wrote down. That person can be real or imaginary.

12. Let this person tell you how he or she would handle the situation.

13. Listen to this person's words. As soon as you begin getting the drift of his or her message, turn off the CD and start writing it down. Write without stopping for at least five minutes.

EXERCISE 6, PART I

1. Sit comfortably in your chair, with your hands clasped or palms touching in your lap.

2. Close your eyes and again breathe out three times.

3. As I name the chakras, bring your energy up from the base of your spine with each inhalation, and then exhale.

4. Now bring your breath and your attention to the base of your spine, your first chakra, the gonads. Feel the energy swirling there, perfectly balanced...and exhale.

5. Now bring your breath and your attention from the base of your spine to about an inch or so below your navel, your second chakra, the cells of Leydig. Feel the energy swirling there, perfectly balanced with the one below...and exhale.

6. Now bring your breath and your attention from the base of your spine to your solar plexus, your third chakra, the adrenal glands. Feel the energy swirling there, perfectly balanced with the two below...and exhale.

7. Now bring your breath and your attention from the base of your spine to the center of your chest, your fourth chakra, the heart chakra, the thymus gland. Feel the energy swirling there, perfectly balanced with the three below...and exhale.

8. Now bring your breath and your attention from the base of your spine to the base of your throat, your fifth chakra, the thyroid gland. Feel the energy swirling there, perfectly balanced with the four below...and exhale.

9. Now bring your breath and your attention from the base of your spine to the crown of your head, the sixth chakra, the pineal gland. Feel the energy swirling there, perfectly balanced with the five below...and exhale.

10. And now let your breath and your attention soar from the base of your spine to the crown of your head and flow down to your third eye, between your eyebrows, your seventh chakra, the pituitary gland. Feel the energy swirling there, perfectly balanced with the six others...and exhale.

11. As you feel these energy centers pulsing, with energy flowing through your body, sense which chakra you would connect or associate with the safe haven you created earlier.

Continued on next page

12. Bring your consciousness to this energy center and sit with it for a while, as if its energy were a pulse and you are sitting in the pulsation, quietly pulsing with it....

13. Now, without opening your eyes, think of someone (a person) or something (a thing, a situation, or a process) that is very important to your life.

14. Picture that person, process, thing, or situation in your mind's eye.

15. Now very slowly, in a very relaxed way, let your inner eye move to the right of that picture and see what is there. (Do not judge or interpret it, just see it.)

16. Now bring your mind's eye back to the central picture.

17. Let your inner eye now see what is to the left of the picture.

18. When you have all three images, keep the CD playing, open your eyes, and write down the three images.

> ### Helpful Hint
>
> Some of you may believe, as I once did, that you can't see anything with your eyes closed. Although you try looking, all you see is blackness—or nothing. In that case, simply hear a word, or let your mind give you a word. Seeing an image is not as important as knowing what the person or object is. So if you can't yet visualize or don't think you do it well, relax. You have other ways of finding the right and left images.
>
> If, after trying again, you still see nothing on one side or blank spaces on both sides, that's okay. As the exercise continues, you'll work with the blankness, instead of with other images.

19. Now close your eyes again and breathe out three times.

20. In the stillness of yourself, choose a favorite color and visualize it all around you, like a huge cloud.

21. Breathe slowly and evenly, allowing yourself to bathe in the color and whatever that color means to you. Let the color relax and soothe you....

22. Now, with your eyes still closed, see the central image again in your mind's eye.

Continued on next page

23. Allow this image to turn into a symbol (the way a dove is a symbol for peace). Remember that whatever symbol appears is the right one for this exercise.

24. Keeping your eyes closed, hold the symbol in the center of your inner vision and see again the images on the right and on the left.

25. Keep looking at all three images—the right, the central symbol, and the left—until you see or understand a relationship that links them.

26. When you understand the relationship, open your eyes but write nothing down. Instead, play track #3 of the CD. (If, however, you cannot find a relationship, don't struggle. Just play track #3.)

1. To finish this exercise, you are going to write about this relationship you saw and what it means to you—but *not* in the form of a personal essay. Instead, you are going to invent an observer from another planet—a Martian—who has to explain this weird relationship to its leaders.

    In other words, as you write, you will be seeing the relationship as global, not personal. It is now part of a world pattern. It is now part of, or representative of, all humanity.

    The important phrase here is *part of*. In this piece of writing, you will leave behind your personalized focus and see whatever was so personally meaningful to you as *part of the world*—*part of* something bigger than yourself.

    Your Martian can be as serious, as inventive, or as playful as you wish—or as your Martian wishes.... For any of you who found no relationship connecting the images, simply have your Martian indicate that lack of understanding in its report to its leaders.

2. Now breathe out again three times.

3. Imagine a Martian, any way you want.

4. Hear or imagine what the Martian is saying about the relationship linking the three images.

5. As soon as you can "hear" the Martian begin speaking (in your language, of course), open your eyes, turn off the CD, and write down what the Martian has to say.

EXERCISE 6A, PART I

1. Sit comfortably in a your chair, with your hands clasped or palms touching in your lap.

2. Close your eyes and again breathe out three times.

3. As I name the chakras, bring your energy up from the base of your spine with each inhalation, and then exhale.

4. Now bring your breath and your attention to the base of your spine, your first chakra, the gonads. Feel the energy swirling there, perfectly balanced...and exhale.

5. Now bring your breath and your attention from the base of your spine to about an inch or so below your navel, your second chakra, the cells of Leydig. Feel the energy swirling there, perfectly balanced with the one below...and exhale.

6. Now bring your breath and your attention from the base of your spine to your solar plexus, your third chakra, the adrenal glands. Feel the energy swirling there, perfectly balanced with the two below...and exhale.

7. Now bring your breath and your attention from the base of your spine to the center of your chest, your fourth chakra, the heart chakra, the thymus gland. Feel the energy swirling there, perfectly balanced with the three below...and exhale.

8. Now bring your breath and your attention from the base of your spine to the base of your throat, your fifth chakra, the thyroid gland. Feel the energy swirling there, perfectly balanced with the four below...and exhale.

9. Now bring your breath and your attention from the base of your spine to the crown of your head, the sixth chakra, the pineal gland. Feel the energy swirling there, perfectly balanced with the five below...and exhale.

10. And now let your breath and your attention soar from the base of your spine to the crown of your head and flow down to your third eye, between your eyebrows, your seventh chakra, the pituitary gland. Feel the energy swirling there, perfectly balanced with the six others...and exhale.

11. As you feel these energy centers pulsing, with energy flowing through your body, sense which chakra you would connect or associate with the safe haven you created earlier.

Continued on next page

12. Bring your consciousness to this energy center and sit with it for a while, as if its energy were a pulse and you are sitting in the pulsation, quietly pulsing with it....

13. Now, without opening your eyes, think of someone (a person) or something (a thing, a situation, or a process) that is very important to your life.

14. Picture that person, process, thing, or situation in your mind's eye.

15. Now very slowly, in a very relaxed way, let your inner eye move to the right of that picture and see what is there. (Do not judge or interpret it, just see it.)

16. Now look to the right of that and see what is there.

17. Now bring your mind's eye back to the central picture.

18. Let your inner eye now see what is to the left of the picture.

19. Now look to the left of that, and see what is there.

20. When you have all five images, keep the CD playing, open your eyes, and and write down the five images.

21. Now close your eyes again and breathe out three times.

22. In the stillness of yourself, choose a favorite color and visualize it all around you, like a huge cloud.

23. Breathe slowly and evenly, allowing yourself to bathe in the color and whatever that color means to you. Let the color relax and soothe you....

24. Now, with your eyes still closed, see the central image again in your mind's eye.

25. Allow this image to turn into a symbol (the way a dove is a symbol for peace). Remember that whatever symbol appears is the right one for this exercise.

26. Keeping your eyes closed, hold the symbol in the center of your inner vision and see again the images on the right and the right and on the left and the left.

27. Keep looking at all five images—the two on the right, the central symbol, and the two on the left—until you see or understand a relationship that links them.

28. When you understand the relationship, open your eyes but write nothing down. Instead, play track #5 of the CD. (If, however, you cannot find a relationship, don't struggle. Just play track #5.)

Exercise 6A, part II

1. To finish this exercise, you are going to write about this relationship you saw and what it means to you—but *not* in the form of a personal essay. Instead, you are going to invent an observer from another planet—a Martian—who has to explain this weird relationship to its leaders.

   In other words, as you write, you will be seeing the relationship as global, not personal. It is now part of a world pattern. It is now part of, or representative of, all humanity.

   The important phrase here is *part of*. In this piece of writing, you will leave behind your personalized focus and see whatever was so personally meaningful to you as *part of the world*—*part of* something bigger than yourself.

   Your Martian can be as serious, as inventive, or as playful as you wish—or as your Martian wishes. . . . For any of you who found no relationship connecting the images, simply have your Martian indicate that lack of understanding in its report to its leaders.

2. Now breathe out again three times.

3. Imagine a Martian, any way you want.

4. Hear or imagine what the Martian is saying about the relationship linking the five images.

5. As soon as you can "hear" the Martian begin speaking (in your language, of course), open your eyes, turn off the CD, and write down what the Martian has to say.

EXERCISE 7

track 6 on the CD

1. You will start again by balancing your energies, so close your eyes and breathe out again three times.

2. Now bring your breath and your attention to the base of your spine, your first chakra, the gonads. Feel the energy swirling there, perfectly balanced...and exhale.

3. Now bring your breath and your attention from the base of your spine to about an inch or so below your navel, your second chakra, the cells of Leydig. Feel the energy swirling there, perfectly balanced with the one below...and exhale.

4. Now bring your breath and your attention from the base of your spine to your solar plexus, your third chakra, the adrenal glands. Feel the energy swirling there, perfectly balanced with the two below...and exhale.

5. Now bring your breath and your attention from the base of your spine to the center of your chest, your fourth chakra, the heart chakra, the thymus gland. Feel the energy swirling there, perfectly balanced with the three below...and exhale.

6. Now bring your breath and your attention from the base of your spine to the base of your throat, your fifth chakra, the thyroid gland. Feel the energy swirling there, perfectly balanced with the four below...and exhale.

7. Now bring your breath and your attention from the base of your spine to the crown of your head, the sixth chakra, the pineal gland. Feel the energy swirling there, perfectly balanced with the five below...and exhale.

8. And now let your breath and your attention soar from the base of your spine to the crown of your head and flow down to your third eye, between your eyebrows, your seventh chakra, the pituitary gland. Feel the energy swirling there, perfectly balanced with the six others...and exhale.

9. Feel the energy flowing, balanced, throughout your entire body.

10. Now return to the room that you furnished with your beliefs about yourself. See it clearly in your mind's eye.

Continued on next page

11. Rearrange the furniture in the room as you think fit.

- Replace or weed out any pieces that no longer belong.
- Re-size any items that are too big or too small for their presence in your life.

12. When you have created a room in which you are comfortable, in which you can see yourself sitting and relaxing, open your eyes, turn off the CD, and write down all the changes that you made.

EXERCISE 7A

track 7 on the CD

1. Close your eyes and breathe out again three times.

2. Return to your laboratory, and picture yourself in it.

3. Choose whatever seems to be the right seat in the room—or the right place—for asking your question.

4. Sit, stand, or lie down in that place, whichever makes you most comfortable.

5. Close your eyes in the room of the self as well.

6. Now state your question, and ask your soul for the answer.

7. Listen until the answer comes.

8. As soon as you have heard the answer, open your eyes, turn off the CD, and write it down.

EXERCISE 7B

1. Close your eyes and breathe out again three times.

2. Return to your room, and picture yourself in it.

3. Choose whatever seems to be the right seat in the room—or the right place—for asking your soul *for* a question.

4. Sit, stand, or lie down in that place, whichever makes you most comfortable.

5. Close your eyes in the room of the self as well.

6. Now ask your soul for the question that you need to be asking.

7. Listen until you hear a question. (No matter how odd it may sound, the first question you hear is the right one for this exercise.)

8. Thank your soul for the question. Then ask the question.

9. Listen until the answer comes.

10. As soon as you have heard the answer, open your eyes, turn off the CD, and write it down.

1. You will start again by balancing your energies, so close your eyes and breathe out again three times.

2. Now bring your breath and your attention to the base of your spine, your first chakra, the gonads. Feel the energy swirling there, perfectly balanced...and exhale.

3. Now bring your breath and your attention from the base of your spine to about an inch or so below your navel, your second chakra, the cells of Leydig. Feel the energy swirling there, perfectly balanced with the one below...and exhale.

4. Now bring your breath and your attention from the base of your spine to your solar plexus, your third chakra, the adrenal glands. Feel the energy swirling there, perfectly balanced with the two below...and exhale.

5. Now bring your breath and your attention from the base of your spine to the center of your chest, your fourth chakra, the heart chakra, the thymus gland. Feel the energy swirling there, perfectly balanced with the three below...and exhale.

6. Now bring your breath and your attention from the base of your spine to the base of your throat, your fifth chakra, the thyroid gland. Feel the energy swirling there, perfectly balanced with the four below...and exhale.

7. Now bring your breath and your attention from the base of your spine to the crown of your head, the sixth chakra, the pineal gland. Feel the energy swirling there, perfectly balanced with the five below...and exhale.

8. And now let your breath and your attention soar from the base of your spine to the crown of your head and flow down to your third eye, between your eyebrows, your seventh chakra, the pituitary gland. Feel the energy swirling there, perfectly balanced with the six others...and exhale.

9. Feel the energy flowing, balanced, throughout your entire body.

Continued on next page

10. Now bring your attention to your fourth chakra, the heart chakra, in the center of your chest. Feel the pulsing energy of the heart—of gratitude, appreciation, and love. Sit in your heart, feeling total appreciation for everything you have in your life. Feel the love you have for others. Feel grateful for all the love that others have given you and continue to give you. Stay in the warmth of the love. Sit quietly with the feelings of your heart....

11. [a few minutes later] Stay with the love. Keep feeling the love, the gratitude, the appreciation of everything that is good in your life....

12. [perhaps a minute later] Stay with the love. Feel grateful for everything. Feel all the love inside of you, the love coming into you and the love pouring out from you....

13. [after a full five minutes] Now let your attention and your energy soar to the seventh chakra, the third eye, the pituitary gland. Feel the energy, violet and pulsing. Focus on the pulsing. Pulse in harmony with the third eye until you can feel the pulsation as a part of you....

14. ...As you pulse, pay attention to anything you may see, feel, or hear. When you have seen or heard or felt something, open your eyes. But as you open them, stay with the pulsing, so that you are still focusing from the third eye even though your physical eyes are open.

15. Then turn off the CD and write about what you experienced.

STEPS FOR REBALANCING

1. You need to balance your energies, so close your eyes and breathe out again three times.

2. Now bring your breath and your attention to the base of your spine, your first chakra, the gonads. Feel the energy swirling there, perfectly balanced, not too open, not too closed...and exhale.

3. Now bring your breath and your attention from the base of your spine to about an inch or so below your navel, your second chakra, the cells of Leydig. Feel the energy swirling there, not too open, not too closed, perfectly balanced with the one below... and exhale.

4. Now bring your breath and your attention from the base of your spine to your solar plexus, your third chakra, the adrenal glands. Feel the energy swirling there, not too open, not too closed perfectly balanced with the two below...and exhale.

5. Now bring your breath and your attention from the base of your spine to the center of your chest, your fourth chakra, the heart chakra, the thymus gland. Feel the energy swirling there, not too open, not too closed, perfectly balanced with the three below... and exhale.

6. Now bring your breath and your attention from the base of your spine to the base of your throat, your fifth chakra, the thyroid gland. Feel the energy swirling there, not too open, not too closed, perfectly balanced with the four below...and exhale.

7. Now bring your breath and your attention from the base of your spine to the crown of your head, the sixth chakra, the pineal gland. Feel the energy swirling there, not too open, not too closed, perfectly balanced with the five below...and exhale.

8. And now let your breath and your attention soar from the base of your spine to the crown of your head and flow down to your third eye, between your eyebrows, your seventh chakra, the pituitary gland. Feel the energy swirling there, not too open, not too closed, perfectly balanced with the six others...and exhale.

9. Feel the energy flowing, fully balanced, throughout your entire body.

Continued on next page

10. When you are ready, open your eyes.

11. Stand up and stretch.

12. Now turn off the CD and get something healthy and grounding to eat, whether a piece of fruit or some sort of protein, perhaps along with a glass of water or a cup of herbal tea.

Praise for Natalie Reid's Workshops

"It was as if all my previous work had been to empty myself of everything that wasn't real, so that I could come to this workshop and be totally filled with what is real and true about myself."
— Ann G., *Tiburon, CA*

"I came away with a clear roadmap for the next section of my life."
— Judith P., *Duanesburg, NY*

"The workshop with Natalie assured me that I am connected with the universe and doing what I am supposed to be doing, wherever the opportunity presents itself."
— Carol P., *Burtonsville, MD*

"Your workshop offers a unique and innovative approach to divine expression."
— Michael D., *Eugene, OR*

"Natalie Reid is an architect of rooms of the mind."
— Linda H., *Columbus, OH*

"I loved the exercises because they bypassed our head. They simply led us into our own inner world and the stories that live there—not fictional stories. True stories. The stories that guide us and shape our lives. Thank you for that gift."
— Marian G., *Boston, MA*

"Natalie's work is wonderfully playful and powerfully supportive of where I am in my own creative and spiritual process. Her mystical voice, wedded with very practical tools and unusual techniques, helped shift my view of my life "as is" and the possibilities for change."
— Yael F., *Washington, DC*

"The exercises in your workshops are powerful, as they bring up a lot of hidden or unconscious material. Your gentle way of helping people to cope with what they have uncovered is what makes you special. From the beginning, when you spoke about the work involved, the sincerity and dedication to that unfolding that was in your voice appealed to many, including me. The work begun with you was a further unfolding of the soulfulness to which I aspire."
— Claudette W., *Bayside, NY*

"The workshop spoke to a part of me that hadn't been 'fed' in a long time."
— **Joann G.**, *Alexandria, VA*

"I now see that what people do with the results of what they write in your workshop is that every word, every single syllable, is potentially (and literally) the key to their life."
— **Rasma H.**, *Madison, WI*

"Natalie Reid's new workshop offers an immensely safe space. In addition to the brilliant information she provides and the journey experiences she creates for her voyagers, one of the things that makes it so powerful and effective is Natalie's overall emphasis on the participants' well being."
— **Paula M.**, *Oradell, NJ*

"You created a very safe non-judgemental atmosphere, which was very important and very liberating."
— **Monica B.**, *London, UK*

"Natalie Reid is a wise woman who helps others look inside and find the riches within. She creates a supportive environment where you can face the darkness and walk through it secure that you will get to the other side. She helps bring you to a greater understanding of who you are and what you need to flourish. She helped me unmask my true self and understand how my life is part of the broader human story. You cannot read her work or take one of her workshops without being touched profoundly by the experience."
— **Leslie N.**, *Niskayuna, NY*

"Natalie is the best at nourishing and nurturing tools to draw out spirit-centered writing. She takes you into your own inner, mythic realms, to infinitely access and create from."
— **Jen K.**, *Santa Fe, NM*

"Natalie Reid is the Alchemist of Soul-chitecture. Her powerful workshop led me on a heroine's journey through the many rooms of my own soul. Natalie gently opened all the doors and gave me the courage and strength to cross thresholds, and to begin the awesome process of honoring each room's intention."
— **Anne S.**, *Kerrville, TX*

"Thanks again for being such an open and nurturing guide during the workshop. The way you live your life fuels me with the courage to evolve more boldly!"
— **Stacey M.**, *Queensbury, NY*

About the Author

Steeped in the Jewish mystical tradition, Natalie Reid (M.A.) for over 10 years has conducted transformational workshops centered on the confluence of creativity, self-awareness, and spirituality. In addition to *The Spiritual Alchemist*, these workshops include *Writing in the Mythological Voice: Elevating the Mundane into Myth* and *From Falsehood to Freedom: Writing Our Way out of the Masks We Wear.* Natalie has developed a unique method for using the writing of fiction to heal from a crisis in faith. Since 1998 she has been a workshop director at the annual weeklong conference of the International Women's Writing Guild.

Natalie has been writing since she was six and took delight in words. She is the author of four books published in Tokyo on American English language and culture. Her short fiction, articles, and book reviews have appeared in numerous publications, including *Natural Bridge* and *13th Moon.* Her novel-in-progress investigates the power of dream to alter a woman's relationship with time and space.

Natalie also designs workshops in English language skills for a multinational clientele that has included the Smithsonian Institution and the Peace Corps. She edits books and consults on papers for European scholars in the field of social research and social policy. She also presents at international conferences. When not on the road giving workshops, she enjoys writing and living in New Mexico.

To order more books, to learn about her workshops, or to request a workshop, go to:
www.thespiritualalchemist.com

To contact Natalie directly, email her at:
nataliereid@thespiritualalchemist.com

Online orders: www.thespiritualalchemist.com
Postal orders: Send either a postal money order or a cashier's check to:

> Natalie Reid
> River Daughter Press
> P.O. Box 20396
> Albuquerque, NM 87154-0396

The Spiritual Alchemist: $18.95 per book
NM sales tax: $1.30 per book
Shipping and handling: $4.99 for the first book and $3.99 each
for any additional books.

The Spiritual Alchemist:	$_____	no. of copies _____
NM sales tax:	$_____	
Shipping and handling:	$_____	
Total:	$_____	

Please print or type your name and address clearly below:
Name: _____

Address: _____

City: _____ State: _____ Zip: _____

Telephone: _____

Email address: _____

For inquiries about Natalie Reid's workshop schedule or book tours, or to arrange to have a workshop or booksigning in your area, go to:
   www.thespiritualalchemist.com

or email Natalie at:
   nataliereid@thespiritualalchemist.com